GW00725677

A VOICE
OF SINGING

Thirty-six new hymns
1988-1992
by Timothy Dudley-Smith

Written since the publication of
SONGS OF DELIVERANCE

CODE NO. 780

Hodder & Stoughton
LONDON SYDNEY AUCKLAND TORONTO

Hope Publishing Company
CAROL STREAM, IL 60188

Hodder & Stoughton, Ltd.
47, Bedford Square
London WC1B 3DP
England

Hope Publishing Company
Carol Stream, Illinois 60188, USA

First published in 1993

ISBN
Hodder & Stoughton 0340 59274 5
Hope Publishing Company 0-916642-50-X
Code No. 780
Library of Congress Catalog Card No. 92-074551
Copyright © 1993 Timothy Dudley-Smith
USA Copyright © 1993 Hope Publishing Company, Carol Stream, Illinois 60188
Printed in the United States of America

PROLOGUE

CHRIST IS THE ONE WHO CALLS

Christ is the One who calls,
the One who loved and came,
to whom by right it falls
to bear the highest Name:
    and still today
    our hearts are stirred
    to hear his word
    and walk his way.

Christ is the One who seeks,
to whom our souls are known.
The word of love he speaks
can wake a heart of stone;
    for at that sound
    the blind can see,
    the slave is free,
    the lost are found.

Christ is the One who died,
forsaken and betrayed;
who, mocked and crucified,
the price of pardon paid.
    Our dying Lord,
    what grief and loss,
    what bitter cross,
    our souls restored!

Christ is the One who rose
in glory from the grave,
to share his life with those
whom once he died to save.
    He drew death's sting
    and broke its chains,
    who lives and reigns,
    our risen King.

Christ is the One who sends,
his story to declare;
who calls his servants friends
and gives them news to share.
    His truth proclaim
    in all the earth,
    his matchless worth
    and saving Name.

A Note on this text appears on page 48.

A © 1993 in A VOICE OF SINGING by Hope Publishing Company, Carol Stream, IL 60188
orld outside USA © 1992 by Timothy Dudley-Smith

'...with a voice of singing,
tell it to the ends of the earth;
the Lord has set his people free.'

Isaiah 48.20

from the version used for Easter 5 in the
Alternative Service Book 1980 of the Church of England.

CONTENTS

The two indexes marked 'cumulative' above refer not only to this collection, but also to texts found in *Lift Every Heart* and in *Songs of Deliverance*. They thus form a complete subject index, and a complete index of first lines, to all my hymn texts up to August 1992.

TDS

FOREWORD

It was said of King Solomon that 'he uttered three thousand proverbs; and his songs were a thousand a five.'[1] This seems a considerable output, but Frank Baker has calculated that Charles Wesley was vastly more prolific. He wrote about 9,000 texts (a figure which takes no account of the often difficult distinction between his verse and his hymns): 'Taking the average... ten lines of verse every day for fifty years, completing an extant poem every other day.'[2]

Such facility is not without its critics. Professor Saintsbury may have had his tongue in his cheek when calling this 'a sin of excess',[3] but Robert Bridges, who thought like a musician even when wearing the garland of Poet Laureate, was positively scathing: 'One must wish that Charles Wesley...had, instead of reeling off all this stuff, concentrated his efforts to produce only what should be worthy of his talents...'[4]. Fortunately George Sampson, editor and literary historian, was not afraid to contradict both these viewpoints: 'Let us rather say that here is God's plenty, from which we may choose as much or as little as we wish.'[5]

'More', of course, can often mean 'worse'. A. C. Benson, who supplied the lyric, 'Land of hope and glory', to Elgar's *Pomp and Circumstance March No 1*, wrote a good many hymns all of which seem to have passed totally into oblivion. David Newsome says of him:

> 'The medium that came most easily to him was verse. Even he had to admit that he amazed himself at the rapidity with which he could produce an ode, a lyric, a sonnet practically to order. Asked to compose an Ode for the thousandth number of the Eton *Chronicle*, Arthur set to at once. "It is odd what an extraordinary facility and rapidity I have for this kind of thing", he commented afterwards. "I wrote it in about ten minutes - and though it is not *good*, it is not bad at all".'[6]

To compare great things with small, this modest collection can claim no such facility, but represents an average of some nine texts a year over the four years since its predecessor - and for me, that feels about right. Most of these texts, as can be seen from the notes, were written during our family holiday in Cornwall each August, at the small house 'Seacroft' which we owned from 1969 to 1991 in Ruan Minor on the Lizard peninsular. A few are marked 'Bramerton' which was my home for 18 years, as Archdeacon of Norwich and then Bishop of Thetford, in a gracious country parsonage (the former Rectory of the village of Bramerton) some six miles from Norwich in East Anglia. The most recent texts were written at Ford, a tiny community on the edge of Salisbury to which we retired in January 1992. Erik Routley wrote a tune which he called RECTORY MEADOW after the name of our home in Bramerton; and Charles Cleall has already given the name ASHLANDS to his new tune to 'Here is the centre' (page 21) after the address of our house in Ford.

In spite of its subtitle, this collection now contains thirty-seven texts, not thirty-six. 'Christ is the One who calls' was only completed after the book was with the publishers, but its theme seems so appropriate to the verse from Isaiah which provides my title that I have added this text as an opening prologue. It is however included in the Notes, indexes etc, in the same way as the thirty-six texts which form the body of the book.

Eight or nine texts a year, or thereabouts, has been my average for the last twenty years. Before that, the figure was much less and more erratic. Of these 197 texts the majority are to be found in *Lift Every Heart*, with a further 36 texts in *Songs of Deliverance*.[7] This present collection follows the pattern of those earlier books; and a sentence or two from the Foreword to *Songs of Deliverance* applies equally here:

'I have followed the same principles of arrangement, indexing and so on as in my earlier collection; and have not repeated here what I said there about various issues in contemporary hymnody - my practice over 'inclusive' or archaic language for example. Similarly, the index of biblical references includes, as before, only those passages which form the substantial basis of a hymn and does not set out to be a comprehensive list of biblical allusions or brief quotations.

(This collection)...is intended as a source book for editors and composers and those interested in comtemporary hymnody; while making available to the more general reader texts which, with some exceptions, cannot at present be found elsewhere.'

One or two correspondents expressed regret that the Notes in *Songs of Deliverance* were generally briefer than in my original collection; and I have therefore deliberately included a few longer and more discursive notes in this book. But my hope is still to publish a definitive collection of my texts, God willing, perhaps about the time of my 70th birthday, some fifty years after the writing of my earliest published hymn text.[8]

But since such a book (if it is ever published) is still some years in the future, I have included towards the end of this book two 'cumulative indexes' - that is, indexes including all my published hymn texts to date, in whichever of my three collections they appear. These offer, therefore, a complete index of first lines; and also a subject index which I hope may be of use to hymnal editors and others in search of texts on a particular theme.

Hymn writing has put me in touch with a wide circle of friends and correspondents, in this country and elsewhere, including publishers, editors, scholars, composers and (best of all) hymn lovers and hymn singers.[9] To them I express my gratitude; as I do once again to the Reverend F. D. Kidner, my unfailing friend and constructive critic. His musical gifts, biblical scholarship and sense of style have given me both the encouragement and the confidence to persevere with this ministry of hymn writing.

It is now over ten years since my friend George Shorney of the Hope Publishing Company took me under his wing and became responsible for the administration of these texts in the USA and Canada. To him for that happy and continuing association, and to Mr. Dick Douglas of Hodder & Stoughton, I record my gratitude for making possible this further collection.

Timothy Dudley-Smith
Ford, 1992

Notes

1. 1 Kings 4.32.

2. Frank Baker, *Representative Verse of Charles Wesley*, London 1962, p.xi.

3. ibid: quoting from *History of English Prosody*, vol.2, 1923, p.531.

4. Robert Bridges, *A Practical Discourse on some Principles of Hymn-singing*, Oxford 1901, reprinted from the *Journal of Theological Studies*, October 1899.

5. George Sampson, *Seven Essays*, Cambridge 1947. No. vii, 'The Century of Divine Songs', p.220.

6. David Newsome, *On the Edge of Paradise*, London 1980, p.86. A. C. Benson was at that time a master at Eton College.

7. *Lift Every Heart*, Collins, London, and Hope Publishing Company, USA, 1984; *Songs of Deliverance*, Hodder & Stoughton, London, and Hope Publishing Company, USA, 1988. Both books are still in print as this goes to press: see outside back cover.

8. See *Lift Every Heart*, p.220, for the note on 'Had he not loved us'. Verses 2 & 3 were written (not as a hymn) in the late 1940s, but did not appear in print until 1969 nor in a hymnal until 1980.

9. I must make special mention of the Hymn Society of Great Britain and Ireland (Hon.Sec., the Reverend Michael Garland, St Nicholas Rectory, Glebe Fields, Curdworth, Sutton Coldfield, W.Midlands B76 9ES) and of the Hymn Society in the United States and Canada (PO Box 30854, Fort Worth, TX 76129, USA). All who are interested in our heritage of hymnody, and in the worship of Almighty God in song, would find membership rewarding.

THE HYMNS

The hymn texts are not numbered, but are listed in alphabetical order both here and in the Notes (page 45). An index of first lines is included for easy reference at the back of the book (page 92).

ALL OUR DAYS WE WILL BLESS THE LORD

based on Psalm 34

All our days we will bless the Lord,
Bless and hallow his Name adored;
Call together to God most high,
Drawn to him who will hear our cry;
Ever look to him, Lord indeed,
Friend and Father to those in need.

God our refuge, our shield and sword,
He himself is our great reward.
In his service, with love and fear,
Joy be theirs who in faith draw near;
Known and cherished in all their ways,
Life possessing and length of days.

May no lies on our lips be heard,
No dishonouring deed or word;
Over all is the Lord above,
Peace bestowing and steadfast love,
Quick to answer and take our part,
Rich in mercy to heal the heart.

So delivered from hour to hour,
Trusting God and his sovereign power,
Uncondemned at his judgment throne,
Victors ever by grace alone,
We will publish his Name abroad:
All our days we will bless the Lord.

USA © 1993 in A VOICE OF SINGING by Hope Publishing Company, Carol Stream, IL 60188
World outside USA © 1990 by Timothy Dudley-Smith

AS IN THAT UPPER ROOM YOU LEFT YOUR SEAT

As in that upper room you left your seat
and took a towel and chose a servant's part,
so for today, Lord, wash again my feet,
who in your mercy died to cleanse my heart.

I bow before you, all my sin confessed,
to hear again the words of love you said;
and at your table, as your honoured guest,
I take and eat the true and living Bread.

So in remembrance of your life laid down
I come to praise you for your grace divine;
saved by your cross, and subject to your crown,
strengthened for service by this bread and wine.

CHILD OF MARY, NEWLY BORN

Child of Mary, newly born,
   softly in a manger laid,
wake to wonder on this morn,
   view the world your fingers made.
Starlight shone above your bed,
   lantern-light about your birth:
morning sunlight crown your head,
   Light and Life of all the earth!

Child of Mary, grown and strong,
   traveller, teacher, young and free,
see him stride the hills along,
   Christ the Man of Galilee.
Wisdom from a world above
   now by waiting hearts is heard:
hear him speak the words of love,
   Christ the true eternal Word.

Child of Mary, grief and loss,
   all the sum of human woe,
crown of thorn and cruel cross,
   mark the path you choose to go.
Man of sorrows, born to save,
   bearing all our sins and pains:
from his cross and empty grave
   Christ the Lord of glory reigns.

Child of Mary, gift of grace,
   by whose birth shall all be well,
one with us in form and face,
   God with us, Emmanuel!
Night is past and shadows fled,
   wake to joy on Christmas morn:
sunlight crown the Saviour's head,
   Christ the Prince of peace is born.

CHRIST IS COME! LET EARTH ADORE HIM

Christ is come! Let earth adore him;
　　God appears in mortal frame.
Saints and angels bow before him,
　　praise his high and holy Name.
Word of our salvation's story,
　　helpless babe of human birth,
Christ has laid aside his glory,
　　born for us a child of earth.

Christ is come and calls us to him;
　　here by faith behold your King;
with the shepherds kneel to view him,
　　with the wise your treasures bring.
Child today and man tomorrow,
　　by his cross and crown of thorn
he shall vanquish sin and sorrow,
　　sing we then that Christ is born.

Christ is come! Let all enthrone him,
　　every tongue declare his praise;
every heart rejoice to own him
　　King of everlasting days.
Christ is come, our sure salvation,
　　Christ the ransomed sinner's friend,
so with all his new creation
　　sing the song that knows no end.

USA © 1993 in A VOICE OF SINGING by Hope Publishing Company, Carol Stream, IL 60188
World outside USA © 1989 by Timothy Dudley-Smith

CHRIST IS THE BREAD OF LIFE INDEED

based on the seven "I am" passages in St John's Gospel

Christ is the Bread of life indeed
  who nourishes the hungry soul,
the one on whom our spirits feed,
  who makes us whole.

Christ is the Door which open stands,
  the one who watch and ward will keep;
the Shepherd of the heavenly lands
  who knows his sheep.

Christ is the Light of all the earth,
  to end our night of sin and gloom;
the Resurrection-Life, whose birth
  has burst the tomb.

Christ is the living Vine, and we
  abide in him, who hear his call.
The Way, the Truth, the Life is he,
  and Lord of all.

CHRIST THE WAY OF LIFE POSSESS ME

based on four images from the Book of Proverbs

Christ the Way of life possess me,
 lift my heart to love and praise;
guide and keep, sustain and bless me,
 all my days.

Well of life, for ever flowing,
 make my barren soul and bare
like a watered garden growing,
 fresh and fair.

May the Tree of life in splendour
 from its leafy boughs impart
grace divine and healing tender,
 strength of heart.

Path of life before me shining,
 let me come when earth is past,
sorrow, self and sin resigning,
 home at last.

USA © 1993 in A VOICE OF SINGING by Hope Publishing Company, Carol Stream, IL 60188
World outside USA © 1988 by Timothy Dudley-Smith

CHRIST WHO CALLED DISCIPLES TO HIM

Christ who called disciples to him
　　from their nets beside the sea,
taught and trained the twelve who knew him
　　by the shores of Galilee,
　　　　still he calls us to his service,
　　　　saying 'Come and follow me'.

Christ whose touch was life and healing,
　　sight to blind and strength to lame,
deed and word alike revealing
　　mercy evermore the same,
　　　　still he calls us to his service,
　　　　strong in faith to bear his Name.

Christ, in whom for our salvation
　　God's unchanging love is shown,
risen now in exaltation,
　　reigning from the Father's throne,
　　　　still he calls us to his service,
　　　　and to make his gospel known.

Christ whose calling knows no ending,
　　no reserve and no delays,
by his Spirit's power defending
　　those who follow in his ways,
　　　　we are come to be his servants,
　　　　faithful now and all our days.

USA © 1993 in A VOICE OF SINGING by Hope Publishing Company, Carol Stream, IL 60188
World outside USA © 1989 by Timothy Dudley-Smith

COME, WATCH WITH US THIS CHRISTMAS NIGHT

Come, watch with us this Christmas night;
   our hearts must travel far
to darkened hills and heavens bright
with star on shining star;
to where in shadowy silence sleep
   the fields of Bethlehem,
as shepherds wake their watch to keep
and we will watch with them.

Who would not join the angel songs
that tell the Saviour's birth?
The Lord for whom creation longs
has come at last to earth.
The fullness of the Father's love
   is ours at Bethlehem,
while angels throng the skies above
and we will sing with them.

Who would not journey far to share
the wisdom of the wise,
and gaze with them in wonder where
the world's Redeemer lies?
The Lord of all the Lords that are
   is born at Bethlehem,
and kings shall kneel beneath his star
and we will bow with them.

Lift every heart the hymn of praise
that all creation sings;
the angel host its homage pays,
the shepherds and the kings.
For earth and sky with one accord,
   O Child of Bethlehem,
are come to worship Christ the Lord
and we will come with them.

USA © 1993 in A VOICE OF SINGING by Hope Publishing Company, Carol Stream, IL 60188
World outside USA © 1989 by Timothy Dudley-Smith

DRAW NEAR TO GOD, WHOSE STEADFAST LOVE

Draw near to God, whose steadfast love
    no other gods can show,
in all the heights of heaven above,
    in all the earth below.

His timeless truth is ever new,
    his covenant secure,
his mercies as the morning dew,
    while life and breath endure.

Fulfilling all his love's design,
    embracing flesh and birth,
a nature human and divine,
    he came in Christ to earth.

And he whose throne eternal stands
    his Spirit's life imparts,
to share a house not made with hands,
    a home within our hearts.

Have faith in God: his promise claim
    who longs to hear our prayers;
who knows and loves our human frame,
    who knows, and loves, and cares.

USA © 1993 in A VOICE OF SINGING by Hope Publishing Company, Carol Stream, IL 60188
World outside USA © 1992 by Timothy Dudley-Smith

FREELY, FOR THE LOVE HE BEARS US

Freely, for the love he bears us,
  God has made his purpose plain:
Christ has died and Christ is risen,
Christ will come again.

Christ has died, the world's Redeemer,
Lamb of God for sinners slain:
  Christ has died and Christ is risen,
  Christ will come again.

Christ is risen, high-ascended,
Lord of all to rule and reign:
  Christ has died and Christ is risen,
  Christ will come again.

Christ is coming, King of glory,
firmly then the faith maintain:
  Christ has died and Christ is risen,
  Christ will come again.

USA © 1993 in A VOICE OF SINGING by Hope Publishing Company, Carol Stream, IL 60188
World outside USA © 1989 by Timothy Dudley-Smith

GOD IS NOT FAR,
WHOSE THREEFOLD MERCIES SHINE

God is not far, whose threefold mercies shine
about our ways as wisdom judges best:
in grace and love and fellowship divine
he comes as Father, Son and Spirit blest.

God is but One, who ever reigns above.
Deep in the Godhead is his love expressed.
Before he formed us, children of his love,
he loved as Father, Son and Spirit blest.

For God is love, unquenchable and strong;
see in our Saviour love made manifest!
Praises unending to our God belong
who lives as Father, Son and Spirit blest.

USA © 1993 in A VOICE OF SINGING by Hope Publishing Company, Carol Stream, IL 60188
World outside USA © 1989 by Timothy Dudley-Smith

GOD LIES BEYOND US,
THRONED IN LIGHT RESPLENDENT

God lies beyond us, throned in light resplendent,
  Father eternal, source of all creation.
To him in glory, timeless and transcendent,
  High King of Ages, come with adoration.

God walks beside us, born to be our neighbour,
  died to redeem us, risen and ascended;
love to the loveless, friend of all who labour,
  Christ our Companion, till our days are ended.

God lives within us, breath and life instilling,
  daily transforming ways of thought and seeing.
Spirit all-holy, all our spirits filling,
  blow, Wind, about us! Burn within our being.

God in three persons, Trinity of splendour!
  To God the Father, all in all sustaining,
and God the Saviour, adoration render,
  with God the Spirit, One in glory reigning.

USA © 1993 in A VOICE OF SINGING by Hope Publishing Company, Carol Stream, IL 60188
World outside USA © 1989 by Timothy Dudley-Smith

GOD WHOSE LOVE IS EVERYWHERE

The orange,
representing
all the world.

God whose love is everywhere
made our earth and all things fair,
ever keeps them in his care;
    praise the God of love!
He who hung the stars in space
holds the spinning world in place;
    praise the God of love!

The sticks, fruit
& nuts, representing
the four seasons &
the fruit of the
earth.

Come with thankful songs to sing
of the gifts the seasons bring,
summer, winter, autumn, spring;
    praise the God of love!
He who gave us breath and birth
gives us all the fruitful earth;
    praise the God of love!

The red ribbon,
representing the
blood of Christ shed
for us.

Mark what love the Lord displayed,
all our sins upon him laid,
by his blood our ransom paid;
    praise the God of love!
Circled by that scarlet band
all the world is in his hand;
    praise the God of love!

The lighted candle,
representing Christ
the Light of the world.

See the sign of love appear,
flame of glory, bright and clear,
light for all the world is here;
    praise the God of love!
Gloom and darkness, get you gone!
Christ the Light of life has shone;
    praise the God of love!

HERE IS THE CENTRE: STAR ON DISTANT STAR

Here is the centre: star on distant star
shining unheeded in the depths of space,
worlds without number, all the worlds there are,
turn in their travelling to this holy place.
    Here in a stable and an ox's stall
    laid in a manger lies the Lord of all.

Now is the moment: God in flesh appears,
down from the splendours of his throne sublime,
High King of Ages, Lord of all the years,
God everlasting stoops to space and time.
    All that was promised now is brought to birth,
    Jesus our Saviour come at last to earth.

Son of the Father, God's eternal Word,
emptied of glory, born to cross and grave;
ours is the secret ancient prophets heard,
God in our likeness come to seek and save:
    Christ in his passion, bearer of our sins;
    and, from his rising, risen life begins.

Come then rejoicing! Praise be all our songs!
Love lies among us in the stable bare,
light in our darkness, righting of all wrongs,
hope for the future, joy enough to share.
    Peace to our hearts for God is on the throne!
    Christ our Redeemer comes to claim his own.

HOW GREAT OUR GOD'S MAJESTIC NAME!

based on Psalm 8

How great our God's majestic Name!
His glory fills the earth and sky.
His praise the heavenly host proclaim,
eternal God and Lord most high.

His fingers set the moon in place,
the stars their Maker's hand declare;
in earth and sky alike we trace
the pattern of his constant care.

And what of us? Creation's crown,
upheld in God's eternal mind;
on whom he looks in mercy down
for tender love of humankind.

His praise the heavenly host proclaim
and we his children tell his worth:
how great is God's majestic Name,
his glory seen in all the earth!

LET THE EARTH ACCLAIM HIM

based on Psalm 100

Let the earth acclaim him,
　serve the Lord with gladness;
worship him, and name him
　source of all our song.
He it is who made us,
　sought us in our sadness,
and in joy arrayed us
　who to him belong.

Come then with thanksgiving,
　God on high confessing:
Lord of all things living,
　fill his courts with praise.
Come in faith, securing
　everlasting blessing:
loved by Love enduring
　to eternal days.

LORD, FOR THE GIFT OF THIS NEW DAY

Lord, for the gift of this new day
  receive alike our praise and prayer,
that all we think and do and say
    be in your care.

Our minds be set on things of worth,
    things excellent and good and true;
so may we love not only earth
    but heaven too.

Our actions match the faith we claim,
    integrity attend our ways;
let all be done in Jesus' Name
    and to his praise.

Our speech express a heart renewed
    and lightened by the Spirit's love,
with words of grace and truth endued
    from God above.

So may your benediction rest
    on us and all we meet this day,
who walk with Jesus, doubly blest,
    the pilgrim way.

LORD, HEAR US AS WE PRAY

suitable for a marriage

Lord, hear us as we pray,
   a Father's blessing give,
that Christ be light upon our way
   and truth by which to live.

A faith in which to rest,
   a living hope, impart;
with charity of spirit blest
   in humbleness of heart.

The Spirit from above
   his gracious gifts increase,
that Christ be all our joy and love
   as Christ is all our peace.

LORD OF OUR LIVES, OUR BIRTH AND BREATH

Suitable for a funeral

Lord of our lives, our birth and breath,
    the measure of our days,
to you alone, in life and death,
    we bring our prayer and praise.

For love of life and all its powers
    by sunlit memory stored,
for tasted joys and timeless hours,
    we praise our living Lord.

Within the love of Christ we rest
    whose cross is strong to save,
by whose eternal hand possessed
    we fear not death or grave.

So move our hearts, O God above,
    by whom all gifts are given,
that one in Christ with those we love
    we walk with him to heaven.

MY DAYS OF WAITING ENDED

based on Psalm 40. 1 - 3

My days of waiting ended,
the Lord has heard my cry,
and in his grace befriended
a prisoner left to die.
The pit was all around me,
the mire and shifting sand,
but God in mercy found me
a rock on which to stand.

To God our strong salvation
eternal praise belongs,
with ceaseless celebration
and new triumphant songs.
Let all his saints adore him,
who trust in God alone;
lift high your hearts before him
and make his mercies known.

USA © 1993 in A VOICE OF SINGING by Hope Publishing Company, Carol Stream, IL 60188
World outside USA © 1989 by Timothy Dudley-Smith

NOW IS CHRIST RISEN FROM THE DEAD

Now is Christ risen from the dead,
    now are the powers of darkness fled,
    Alleluia...
Gone is the night of sin and gloom,
Jesus is risen from the tomb.
    Alleluia...

Now is Christ risen from the dead,
empty there lies his narrow bed,
    Alleluia...
Christ and his cross have won the day;
come, see the grave in which he lay.
    Alleluia...

Now is Christ risen from the dead,
he who his blood for sinners shed,
    Alleluia...
In him who died to bear our sins
our resurrection-life begins.
    Alleluia...

Now is Christ risen from the dead,
risen and reigning as he said,
    Alleluia...
Praise him who light and life restored,
Praise him, our ever-living Lord!
    Alleluia...

USA © 1993 in A VOICE OF SINGING by Hope Publishing Company, Carol Stream, IL 60188
World outside USA © 1992 by Timothy Dudley-Smith

O GOD OF EVERLASTING LIGHT

based on John 3.3-16

O God of everlasting light,
   whose boundless kingdom lies
beyond our world of sense and sight,
   unseen by mortal eyes;
we long to learn what Jesus taught
   that from this dust of earth
the seeking soul may still be brought
   a second time to birth.

Here may the springing waters flow
   to cleanse from every stain;
here may the Wind of heaven blow
   to stir to life again.
So freed from all the powers of death,
   from all our secret sins,
and quickened by the Spirit's breath,
   our life in Christ begins.

O God of love, your Son you gave,
   we see him lifted high;
your Son, who came to seek and save
   and on the cross to die.
We name him Lord of life and love
   with all our ransomed powers,
for born anew from God above
   eternal life is ours.

O GOD WHO BROUGHT THE LIGHT TO BIRTH

a meditation on Genesis 1 - 3

O God who brought the light to birth,
    the moon and all the starry skies,
who set in space the globe of earth
    and made the sun in splendour rise,
        teach us to love the light, we pray,
        and walk as children of the day.

A fertile earth, a sky and sea,
    you filled with creatures great and small,
and fashioned humankind to be
    your own vice-regents over all:
        teach us your fragile world to tend,
        and live as all creation's friend.

Delight and purpose, work and rest,
    and innocence a garden made,
with human love and marriage blest,
    before the flowers began to fade:
        teach us your purpose to fulfil
        and find delight within your will.

What sin was theirs who fell from grace
    enslaved by one forbidden tree,
to found a fallen human race
    no longer unashamed and free:
        teach us to flee from Satan's power
        and keep us in temptation's hour.

For Christ has crushed the serpent's head
    to put an end to griefs and sins;
through him the powers of death are dead
    and resurrection life begins:
        teach us to make his triumphs plain,
        and in him live, and rise, and reign.

O GOD WHOSE THOUGHTS ARE NOT AS OURS

O God whose thoughts are not as ours,
   whose word can bring to birth
a universe of nature's powers,
   a green and ordered earth;
beyond the frame of time and space
   we lift our spirits' gaze,
and at the heart of all we trace
   the edges of your ways.

The God of thunder, fire and flame,
   whose voice the prophets heard;
creation trembles at his Name
   and bows before his word.
The sum of things is in his hands
   whom sun and stars confess;
beyond the clouds of heaven stands
   a throne of righteousness.

O God of love, whose love is shown
   to all your hand has made,
the likeness of your glory known
   when mists and shadows fade:
the light of God's eternal light
   in Christ be shed abroad,
to shine upon our mortal sight,
   the vision of the Lord.

USA © 1993 in A VOICE OF SINGING by Hope Publishing Company, Carol Stream, IL 60188
World outside USA © 1988 by Timothy Dudley-Smith

PEACE BE YOURS AND DREAMLESS SLUMBER

Peace be yours and dreamless slumber,
heaven's King
come to bring
blessings without number.

Helpless now in love's surrender,
by your birth,
Child of earth,
emptied of all splendour!

Dearest Jesus! So we name you,
born to save;
cross and grave
soon will come to claim you.

Then to heaven's throne ascended!
All our tears,
wasted years,
sins and sorrows ended.

Sing we then, O Saviour sleeping,
our Noel,
all is well,
in the Father's keeping.

USA © 1993 in A VOICE OF SINGING by Hope Publishing Company, Carol Stream, IL 60188
World outside USA © 1989 by Timothy Dudley-Smith

SO THE DAY DAWN FOR ME

So the day dawn for me,
　　so the day break,
Christ watching over me,
Christ as I wake.

Be the day shine to me,
be the day bright,
Christ my companion be,
Christ be my light.

Be the day dark to me,
be the day drear,
Christ shall my comfort be,
Christ be my cheer.

Be the day swift to me,
be the day long,
Christ my contentment be,
Christ be my song.

So the day close for me,
so the night fall,
Christ watching over me,
Christ be my all.

THE BEST OF GIFTS IS OURS

based on Philippians 4. 4-9

The best of gifts is ours
within our Father's hand,
with joy and peace beyond the powers
of mind to understand.

Bid every anxious care
and wayward thought depart;
make known your need to God in prayer
and he will keep your heart.

Give love the highest place;
have all things good your goal.
Let truth and righteousness and grace
in peace possess your soul.

In honour take delight;
let justice mark your ways;
things innocent and pure and right
command your love and praise.

Become God's garden fair,
where virtue freely flowers;
and as the mind of Christ is there
the God of peace is ours.

USA © 1993 in A VOICE OF SINGING by Hope Publishing Company, Carol Stream, IL 60188
World outside USA © 1990 by Timothy Dudley-Smith

THE CHURCH OF GOD ON EARTH, WE COME

The church of God on earth, we come
   to him whose love has sought us,
a people lost and far from home,
   in Christ he came and bought us.
For all in faith's allegiance sworn
God's new community is born,
   to live as Jesus taught us.

And still the call of God is heard
   that summons all creation.
He sends his Spirit and his word,
   the word of our salvation;
and as the seed of life is sown
so love's community is known
   in every generation.

Within the bond of love and peace,
   the grace of Christ possessing,
we sing the songs that never cease,
   our God and King confessing.
Eternal praise unite our powers
for Christ's community is ours,
   and everlasting blessing.

THE LOVE OF CHRIST, WHO DIED FOR ME

The love of Christ, who died for me,
  is more than mind can know;
his mercy measureless and free
  to meet the debt I owe.

He came my sinful cause to plead,
  he laid his glories by,
for me a homeless life to lead,
  a shameful death to die.

My sins I only see in part,
  my self-regarding ways;
the secret places of my heart
  lie bare before his gaze.

For me the price of sin he paid;
  my sins beyond recall
are all alike on Jesus laid,
  he died to bear them all.

O living Lord of Life, for whom
  the heavens held their breath,
to see, triumphant from the tomb,
  a love that conquers death,

Possess my heart, that it may be
  your kingdom without end,
O Christ who died for love of me,
  and lives to be my friend.

THE PILGRIM CHURCH OF GOD

based on Ephesians 4.13

The pilgrim church of God,
we mount the narrow way,
we tread the path that Jesus trod,
his call obey:
to whom God sent his Son,
on whom the Spirit came,
who in the faith of Christ are one
and in his Name.

His word of life divine
shall light and truth impart,
and with immortal wisdom shine
for mind and heart.
So may we live and grow,
this grace upon us poured,
with heart and mind alike to know
and serve the Lord.

The work of grace fulfill
while life and strength shall last,
sustain your pilgrim people still
till earth be past;
until what grace began
shall win its final way,
and God complete his perfect plan
in endless day.

What though the way we tread
be dark, or faith be dim?
We look to Christ our risen Head
and walk with him.
So lead your children on
in love and truth and grace,
to come where Christ himself has gone
and see his face.

USA © 1993 in A VOICE OF SINGING by Hope Publishing Company, Carol Stream, IL 60188
World outside USA © 1988 by Timothy Dudley-Smith

TO GOD OUR GREAT SALVATION

based on Psalm 145

To God our great salvation
   a triumph-song we raise,
with hymns of adoration
   and everlasting praise.
That Name beyond all naming
   from age to age adored,
we lift on high proclaiming
   the greatness of the Lord.

Declare in song and story
   the wonders we confess,
who hail the King of glory
   the Lord our righteousness.
In loving-kindness caring
   his mercies stand displayed,
forgiving and forbearing
   to all his hand has made.

His kingdom knows no ending,
   enthroned in light sublime,
his sovereign power extending
   beyond all space and time.
To us and all things living
   he comes in word and deed,
forbearing and forgiving,
   to meet us in our need.

The King of all creation
   is near to those who call;
the God of our salvation
   has stooped to save us all.
Lift high your hearts and voices,
   his praises sound again;
in God his earth rejoices
   for evermore. Amen!

USA © 1993 in A VOICE OF SINGING by Hope Publishing Company, Carol Stream, IL 60188
World outside USA © 1988 by Timothy Dudley-Smith

TO GOD WHO GAVE THE SCRIPTURES

To God who gave the scriptures
 we bring our thanks today
for light upon life's journey,
 a lamp to lead the way;
a sword to face the tempter,
 a seed of life divine,
a glimpse of heaven's glory
 upon our souls to shine.

To God who gave the scriptures
 we sing salvation songs,
for laws of truth and judgment
 to right our human wrongs;
a word to stand for ever
 which faith and light imparts,
a fire of love unchanging
 to burn within our hearts.

To God who gave the scriptures
 we come with love and praise
for all the gospel stories
 of Galilean days;
the words of grace and mercy,
 the cross and all its pains,
as now in risen splendour
 the King of glory reigns.

To God who gave the Scriptures
 we turn in faith to find
a taste of honeyed sweetness
 to nourish heart and mind;
the promise of salvation,
 the covenant restored,
the apostolic witness
 that Jesus is the Lord.

To God who gave the scriptures
 we lift our souls in prayer,
for eyes the Spirit opens
 to find the treasures there;
that as we read and ponder
 one voice alone is heard,
the Christ of all the scriptures,
 the true and living Word.

USA © 1993 in A VOICE OF SINGING by Hope Publishing Company, Carol Stream, IL 60188
World outside USA © 1990 by Timothy Dudley-Smith

WE BELIEVE IN GOD THE FATHER

based on the Apostles' Creed

I believe in God,
the Father almighty,
creator of heaven and earth.

I believe in Jesus Christ,
his only Son, our Lord.
He was conceived by the power
of the Holy Spirit
and born of the Virgin Mary.

He suffered under Pontius Pilate,
was crucified,
died, and was buried.
He descended to the dead.

On the third day he rose again.
He ascended into heaven,
and is seated at the right hand
of the Father.
He will come again to judge
the living and the dead.

I believe in the Holy Spirit,
the holy catholic Church,
the communion of saints,
the forgiveness of sins,
the resurrection of the body,
and the life everlasting. Amen.

We believe in God the Father,
God Almighty, by whose plan
earth and heaven sprang to being,
all created things began.
We believe in Christ the Saviour,
Son of God in human frame,
virgin-born, the child of Mary
upon whom the Spirit came.

Christ, who on the cross forsaken,
like a lamb to slaughter led,
suffered under Pontius Pilate,
he descended to the dead.
We believe in Jesus risen,
heaven's king to rule and reign,
to the Father's side ascended
till as judge he comes again.

We believe in God the Spirit;
in one church, below, above;
saints of God in one communion,
one in holiness and love.
So by faith, our sins forgiven,
Christ our Saviour, Lord and Friend,
we shall rise with him in glory
to the life that knows no end.

USA © 1993 in A VOICE OF SINGING by Hope Publishing Company, Carol Stream, IL 60188
World outside USA © 1989 by Timothy Dudley-Smith

WE TURN IN FAITH TO CHRIST
THE LAMB OF GOD

We turn in faith to Christ the Lamb of God
    and in him rest;
he who the path of pain and sorrow trod,
    by sin oppressed.
    Sinless himself, he died to bear our shame
    when to the loveless and the lost he came.

Lord Jesus, bearer of our grief and loss
    and all our sins,
we come to kneel anew beneath that cross
    where life begins:
    that cross of shame become the healing tree
    where we and all your children may be free.

Christ our Redeemer, bringing life to birth
    from death's dark grave,
Saviour and Sovereign over all the earth
    you died to save,
    take now our love, that comes from sins forgiven;
    teach us on earth to live the life of heaven.

WHAT COLOURS GOD HAS MADE

for Rachel

What colours God has made
  in flower and field and tree!
From springing green of leaf and blade
  I learn his love for me.

The summer's yellow sand,
  the blue of sky and sea,
they tell of God their Maker's hand,
  and all his love for me.

The turning autumn leaves,
  the fruit so full and free,
the golden glow of harvest sheaves,
  declare his love for me.

He frames the winter skies,
  his silver stars I see;
he makes the sun in splendour rise,
  the God who cares for me.

So sing my Father's praise,
  the living God is he,
whose colours brighten all our days,
  who loves and cares for me.

USA © 1992 by Hope Publishing Company, Carol Stream, IL 60188
World outside USA © 1990 by Timothy Dudley-Smith

WHEN THE WAY IS HARD TO FIND

When the way is hard to find,
  seeking first the Father's will,
Lord, your promise call to mind,
all your purposes fulfill:
  when the way is hard to find
  lead your pilgrim people still.

Dark beneath a starless sky,
tossing in the wind and tide,
when the seas of life are high,
lost upon an ocean wide,
  dark beneath a starless sky,
  Lord, we look to you to guide.

Wisdom from the living word
shine upon us as we pray;
may the Spirit's voice be heard
in the dark and cloudy day:
  wisdom from the living word
  be the light upon our way.

Faith be strong and doubt depart,
fear and unbelief be gone;
peace possess the anxious heart
where the light of Christ has shone:
  faith be strong and doubt depart,
  lead your pilgrim people on.

USA © 1993 in A VOICE OF SINGING by Hope Publishing Company, Carol Stream, IL 60188
World outside USA © 1988 by Timothy Dudley-Smith

NOTES
ON THE HYMNS

ALL OUR DAYS WE WILL BLESS THE LORD   88 88 88

Based on	Psalm 34
Theme	Confidence & peace; praise & worship
Written	at Ruan Minor, August 1990
Suggested tune	see below

Psalm 34 is one of the treasures of the psalter. An earlier text of mine, based on this psalm is 'Tell his praise in song and story', (*Lift Every Heart* p.143); a much earlier metrical version, 'Through all the changing scenes of life', is among the most enduring of the Tate and Brady paraphrases, first published 1696.

In the Hebrew this psalm is an acrostic, based on the initial letters of the Hebrew alphabet; and I have sought to follow this device. The text can be regarded as a companion-piece to 'All my soul to God I raise' (*Lift Every Heart* p.49) which follows the acrostic pattern of Psalm 25. Though these two texts both have four stanzas, each of six lines, and both omit the letters X, Y and Z, returning to A for the final line, yet they were written eight years apart and in different metres.

There is, as far as I can discover, no suitable published tune to this metre (though it has attracted the attention of one or two gifted composers).The syllable count gives 88 88 88 as indicated above; but the stresses appear to be a particular combination of anapaest, trochee and dactyl.

Many of those who know and love Psalm 34, and nourish their souls from it, are happy to do so with little idea of the original acrostic form. In the same way, I hope that something of the message of the original is conveyed in this paraphrase, over and above the alphabetical sequence.

C. H. Spurgeon is his monumental study of the Psalms, *The Treasury of David* (Vol 2, London 1907 reprint), regrets that of the nine psalms based on acrostics, only one (119) is so identified in the King James version of the Scriptures; and adds 'I do think that the existence of such a remarkable style of composition ought to be indicated in one way or another, and that some useful purposes are served by it being actually reproduced in the translation'. In our own day this has been done in the R. A. Knox version.

AS IN THAT UPPER ROOM YOU LEFT YOUR SEAT   10 10 10 10

Theme	Holy Communion
Written	at Ford, April 1992
Suggested tune	SONG 22 by Orlando Gibbons

The text moves from the Last Supper and the foot washing, to 'the washing of regeneration' (Titus 3.5) in the final line of verse 1. In this sense, every Service of Holy Communion looks back to the full and free forgiveness that is promised to all those who turn to Christ in faith; and at the same time includes elements of confession and forgiveness for the stains of the daily journey in a fallen world.

'True and living Bread' refers to John 6.32 & 51.

CHILD OF MARY, NEWLY BORN   77 77 D

Theme	Christmas
Written	at Ruan Minor, August 1990
Suggested tune	LYNCH'S LULLABY from J. P.Lynch's *Melodies of Ireland* (c.1845) arranged by Donald Davison; *or* MAIDSTONE by Walter Bond Gilbert; *or* ABERYSTWYTH by Joseph Parry
Published in	*New Songs of Praise 6*, 1991 to LYNCH'S LULLABY (with the suggestion of ABERYSTWYTH as an alternative) *The Popular Carol Book*, 1991 to LYNCH'S LULLABY *Anthem* by Austin Lovelace, Kenwood Press Ltd, USA 1991

The tune LYNCH'S LULLABY was first published as a hymn tune in *Irish Church Praise* (APCK/Oxford,1990) to a text of mine, 'Set your troubled hearts at rest' (*Lift Every Heart*, p.139), in an arrangement by Dr Donald Davison, one of the Music Editors of the book. On hearing it, and noting the name LULLABY, I used the tune in writing a hymn for our 1990 family Christmas card, on which Dr Davison and the publishers allowed me to print the music with the words.

The themes of the text are Christ as Light (v.l); Christ as the incarnate Word (v.2); the glory of Christ's cross and resurrection (v.3); and Christ as our peace (v.4), one with us and God with us, bringing joy in reconciliation.

CHRIST IS COME! LET EARTH ADORE HIM   87 87 D

Theme	Christmas
Written	at Ruan Minor, August 1989
Suggested tune	ABBOT'S LEIGH by Cyril Vincent Taylor; *or* ALLELUIA by Samuel Sebastian Wesley

Written for our family Christmas card, 1989. I first heard it sung as the closing hymn at my 'Farewell Service' in Norwich Cathedral, on December 20th 1991, to mark my retirement as Bishop of Thetford.

CHRIST IS THE BREAD OF LIFE INDEED   8884

Based on   the seven 'I am' passages of St John's gospel (6.35;
                    10.7; 10.11,14; 8.12; 11.25; 15.1; 14.6)

Theme   the Lord Jesus Christ

Written   at Bramerton, August 1991

Suggested tune   PORTLAND by Cyril Vincent Taylor; *or*
                    RIPPONDEN by Norman Cocker; *or*
                    ES IST KEIN TAG by Johann David Meyer

To include these seven references in sixteen lines inevitably implies compression. I have sought to give some tiny echo of Christ's teaching upon each of these 'Parables of the Lord's Person'; though to achieve that, 'Lord of all' must be read as referring to John 14.8-11, where Christ identifies his authority with that of the Father.

In stanza 2, I seek to suggest the truth that the Door can be thought of both as open (to allow the sheep to enter and 'to go in and out'); but also as shut to keep them safe.

CHRIST IS THE ONE WHO CALLS   6666 4444

Theme   The call of God; the Lord Jesus Christ; mission &
                    evangelism

Written   at Ford, August 1992

Suggested tune   LOVE UNKNOWN by John Ireland

The text of this hymn is not in the alphabetical section, but printed as the Prologue on page iii.

The Lambeth Conference of 1988 proposed to the worldwide Anglican Communion that the closing years of this millenium be named a 'Decade of Evangelism' with a renewed and united emphasis on making Christ known to the people of his world. As part of this Decade the present Archbishop of Canterbury has arranged to bring back to the UK 'the two Michaels', Bishop Michael Marshall from the United States and Canon Michael Green from Canada, to work in Christian apologetics, teaching, evangelism and mission; initially in the UK and then throughout the

Anglican Communion. This Archbishops' Initiative for the Decade of Evangelism, now named 'Springboard', was launched at a Service in St Paul's Cathedral, London, on 23rd September 1992; and it was for this Service that the Archbishop of Canterbury asked for a new hymn on the theme of mission.

I have not previously written to the tune LOVE UNKNOWN, considering it to be uniquely dedicated to Samuel Crossman's words from which it takes its name. This is not so; and the tune is used in a number of current hymnals to other words. For example in *Hymns Ancient & Modern, New Standard*, it is set to W. Walsham How's 'Thou art the Christ' and to H. C. A. Gaunt's 'Glory to thee, O God', as well as to 'My song is love unknown'. In *Hymns and Psalms* it is used for F. Pratt Green's marriage hymn 'The grace of life is theirs'. In the *Psalter Hymnal* of the Christian Reformed Church, USA, it carries John Quinn's paraphrase of John 15.1-5, 'I am the holy vine'. With some admitted trepidation (for Crossman's hymn is among my personal favourites) I have therefore written to this metre, with Ireland's tune in mind. It does seem to be a fact, on examination of Crossman's text, that after six matchless verses looking to the cross of Christ ('die', v.1; 'his life did spend', v.2; 'Crucify', v.3; 'against him rise', v.4; 'slay', v.5; 'tomb', v.6) there is no comparable affirmation of resurrection. Indeed only the present tense ('This is my Friend') in v.7 speaks of Jesus alive after his passion. I mention this because if a congregation is to sing Ireland's tune, I should be the first to understand if they preferred to sing it to Crossman's words! But I believe that on examination the two texts differ in theme and content more than might at first appear.

CHRIST THE WAY OF LIFE POSSESS ME   87 83

Based on	four images from the Book of Proverbs: 6.23 etc; 10.11; 3.18 etc, 5.6.
Theme	Christian experience & discipleship; pilgrimage
Written	at Ruan Minor, September 1988
Suggested tune	VIGIL by George Thomas Thalben Ball[1]; *or* NONINGTON by David Heywood Grundy; *or* HORNSEY by Samuel Sebastian Wesley
Published in	*Mission Praise* (combined edition), 1990 to a tune by Phil Burt

Compound images with the word 'life' are not uncommon in Scripture, and are found in the Book of Proverbs, in St John's Gospel, in the Book of Revelation, and in other places also. 'Tree of Life', for example, is an image that begins in Genesis and which (in the words of Henri Blocher[2]) 'represents communion with God, the inexhaustible source of life. The communion is made possible by Wisdom...', (see also Revelation 2 and 22). Jesus refers to himself as, 'the Way' in John 14.6; and his words about the 'well of water springing up into everlasting life' (John 4.14) stand behind verse 2. The shining path of verse 4 is the path of the just from Proverbs 4.18, which is also the path of life.

'Watered garden' in verse 2 is from Jeremiah 31.12 (cf. Proverbs 11.25 and Isaiah 58.11).

1. Set as 87 83 in, e.g., *The BBC Hymn Book*, 1951.
2. Henri Blocher, *In the Beginning*, translated by D. G. Preston, IVP 1984.

CHRIST WHO CALLED DISCIPLES TO HIM   87 87 87

Theme	Christian experience & discipleship; church member-ship & confirmation; response to the gospel
Written	at Ruan Minor, August 1989
Suggested tune	RHUDDLAN (Welsh traditional); *or* LINGWOOD by Armstrong Gibbs; *or* REGENT SQUARE by Henry Smart

The four verses follow the sequence of the gospel story, from the calling of the disciples, through the ministry of Jesus to his death 'for our salvation' and his resurrection, and so to the Great Commission and the gift of the Spirit. The word 'defending' in the final verse is an echo of the traditional confirmation prayer of the Church of England: 'Defend, O Lord, your servants with your heavenly grace...'

COME, WATCH WITH US THIS CHRISTMAS NIGHT
86 86 D (DCM)

Theme	Christmas
Written	at Ruan Minor, August 1988
Suggested tune	NOEL (English traditional); *or* KINGSFOLD (traditional); and see below
Published in	*Christian Music*, Autumn 1989, to CHRISTMAS NIGHT by Robin Sheldon *Mission Praise* (combined edition), 1990 to a tune by Phil Burt

The text is based on a simple structure of: watch with the shepherds; wonder with the wise men; rejoice with the angels; worship with all creation. It was written for our family Christmas card, 1988. The tune NOEL already has associations almost exclusively with Christmas (to 'It came upon the midnight clear') so I was pleased to have two new tunes written to this text (see above). But I should still be glad to find a strong under-used tune, already known to congregations; since inevitably Christmas hymns are only sung at annual intervals, and so afford little opportunity to learn new tunes.

DRAW NEAR TO GOD, WHOSE STEADFAST LOVE   86 86 (CM)

Theme	God the Father, the living God; trust in God
Written	at Ford, February 1992
Suggested tune	RICHMOND by Thomas Haweis adapted by Samuel Webbe the younger

The starting point for this text is Solomon's prayer in 1 Kings 8.22-30. In this context, verse 3 can be seen as the Christian answer to Solomon's question: 'But will God indeed dwell on earth?' In the same way the theme of verse 5 (faith in God, his promises and his care for his children) is one of the concerns of Solomon's great prayer.

FREELY, FOR THE LOVE HE BEARS US   87 85

Theme	Faith; the Lord Jesus Christ
Written	at Ruan Minor, August 1989
Suggested tune	GRIFFIN'S BROOK by John Wilson
Published in	*Mission Praise* (combined edition), 1990 to a tune by Phil Burt

The final couplet of each verse is derived directly (with the single addi-tion of the word 'and') from the acclamations which form part of the Eucharistic Prayer in Rite A Holy Communion of *The Alternative Service Book*, 1980 of the Church of England. I had been contemplating for some time their inclusion into a hymn-text; and, turning over in my mind the tune GRIFFIN'S BROOK, I felt that here was a possible match. That tune is set in *Hymns and Psalms*, the Methodist hymn book of 1983, to Kate Barclay Wilkinson's text 'May the mind of Christ my Saviour'.

The repeated acclamation lends itself to variations when sung as a hymn, either antiphonally within a congregation, or with the help of choir or soloist.

GOD IS NOT FAR, WHOSE THREEFOLD MERCIES SHINE

10 10 10 10

Theme	The Holy Trinity
Written	at Bramerton, June 1989; and at Ruan Minor, August 1990
Suggested tune	JULIUS by Martin Shaw; *or* HOBART HIGH by Derek Scott

In May 1989 I was asked by the Hobart High School, Loddon, Norfolk, to write the words of a short cantata, to be sung in the parish church of Holy Trinity, Loddon, in the summer of 1990 to celebrate its 500th anniversary. The cantata, with music by Derek Scott, is entitled *Stone on Stone* (published 1991 by Stainer and Bell, London) and is about a stylized encounter between the builders of a great church, and various members of the community around them. This text, and the one that follows ('God lies beyond us, throned in light resplendent') are two hymn texts derived from this cantata, celebrating respectively God's immanence and transcendence.

The present text takes its middle verse almost directly from the cantata; and verses 1 and 3 were written a year later on holiday in Ruan Minor. Note in verse 1 the allusion to the trinitarian words of 'the Grace' from 2 Corinthians 13.14.

Derek Scott's setting makes, I am told, a highly suitable hymn tune, which he has named in honour of Hobart High School who commissioned the piece and gave it its first performance.

GOD LIES BEYOND US, THRONED IN LIGHT RESPLENDENT

11 11 11 11

Theme	The Holy Trinity
Written	at Bramerton, June 1989; and at Ruan Minor, August 1990
Suggested tune	LODDON by Derek Scott

The origin of this text is described in the note above to the companion piece 'God is not far, whose threefold mercies shine'.

In this case, the first three verses came from *Stone on Stone*, where they are sung respectively (with minor changes, as from singular to plural) by a Watcher of the Heavens, the Tillers of the Fields, and the Searcher of the Soul. The final verse was written to bind the three into a corporate hymn celebrating our own experience of the Triune God, perceived in different ways and at different times as 'beyond', 'beside' and 'within' us.

GOD WHOSE LOVE IS EVERYWHERE   7775 775

Theme	Christingle
Written	at Ruan Minor and at Poldhu Cove, September 1988
Suggested tune	FALLING FIFTHS by Noël Tredinnick
Published in	*Two new hymns in celebration of Christingle*, 1989 to FALLING FIFTHS
	New Songs of Praise 5, 1990 to FALLING FIFTHS
	The Promise of His Glory, 1991 (words only)

The word 'Christingle' is said to mean 'Christ-light'. Christingle Services
have achieved considerable popularity in England through the work of
the Church of England Children's Society, who have linked the old
Moravian tradition of Christingle to the work they are doing for young
people in need. The theme of the Service is thankfulness, and as the congregation offer their gifts to help bring the light of Christ to darkened
lives, they each receive in return a 'Christingle' as a sign of God's love
and goodness to them. The Christingles are made with an orange, to
which fruit and nuts are secured with wooden sticks. Around the orange
is placed a red ribbon, and a small lighted candle surmounts it. The sig-
nificance of each part can be seen from the commentary beside each verse
of the text on p.20. The words were written in response to a request for
hymns on this theme for *New Songs of Praise 5*. The fifth line of the final
verse may call to mind Henry Vaughan's 'Death and darkness, get you
packing', written 300 years ago.

HERE IS THE CENTRE: STAR ON DISTANT STAR
                                                10 10 10 10 10 10

Theme	Christmas
Written	at Bramerton, August 1991
Suggested tune	SONG 1 by Orlando Gibbons; *or*
	ASHLANDS by Charles Cleall; *or*
	HERE AND NOW by Russell Schulz-Widmar
Published in	*New Song*, September 1992 to ASHLANDS

Written for our 1991 family Christmas card (during the first August for 22
years that we were not at Ruan Minor), the theme of this text is the incarnation of Christ as pivotal in space and time - as indeed the use of the

division between BC and AD shows it to be pivotal in human history. Verse 1 has space in mind, with the whole of God's created universe attending to the stable at Bethlehem. Verse 2 takes the same image, but in terms of time-span. Verse 3 celebrates the event, and verse 4 calls us to appropriate rejoicing.

Both the contemporary tunes listed seem to have been written on or soon after reading the text on our Christmas card. HERE AND NOW was sung at the University Church, Austin, Texas on Christmas Eve 1991; and ASHLANDS (named after our new home) was composed in Scotland about a week earlier.

HOW GREAT OUR GOD'S MAJESTIC NAME   88 88 (LM)

Based on	Psalm 8
Theme	Praise & worship; God the Father, the living God; creation
Written	at Ruan Minor and Poldhu Cove, August 1989
Suggested tunes	EISENACH derived from a melody by J. H. Schein; *or* DOVERSDALE by Samuel Stanley; *or* DUKE STREET by John Hatton
Published in	*The Baptist Hymnal* (USA), 1991 to DUKE STREET

The word 'majestic' in the first line follows the RSV translation.

Verse 2 is an attempt to suggest (following F. D. Kidner in his *Psalms 1-72*, IVP 1973) that the right inference from God's ordered heaven 'is not his remoteness but his eye for detail... he planned no meaningless and empty universe but a home for his family.' Hence in reply to 'What is man?' it is proper to answer, not 'a few random atoms' but 'creation's crown.'

LET THE EARTH ACCLAIM HIM   6665 D

Based on	Psalm 100
Theme	Praise & worship; thanksgiving
Written	at Bramerton, August 1991
Suggested tune	none known

Psalm 100 is set as one of the Canticles ('Jubilate Deo') for Morning Prayer in the *Book of Common Prayer* of the Church of England. The metre and rhyming scheme of this brief metrical version are borrowed from a poem by C. S. Lewis, 'Evensong' (C. S. Lewis, *Poems*, London 1964). David Perry's *Hymns and Tunes Indexed* (Croydon, 1980) gives only two tunes for

6665 D, LEMON'S FARM and DAY OF THE SPIRIT (also known by the rather unfortunate title of WHITSUN JINGLE) and neither appears to fit this text. I should be glad of suggestions.

LORD, FOR THE GIFT OF THIS NEW DAY 8884

Theme	Morning
Written	at Bramerton, August 1991
Suggested tune	ES IST KEIN TAG from a melody by Johann Meyer

The structure of the text is drawn from line 3 of the first verse, 'think and do and say', echoed in the following verses which take the themes of mind, action and speech.

'Doubly blessed' in the final verse refers to the privilege both of walking the pilgrim way, and doing so in the company of Christ; but it can be applied also to God's blessing resting both upon ourselves and upon those we meet.

LORD, HEAR US AS WE PRAY 66 86 (SM)

Theme	Peace & blessing; a marriage
Written	at Ruan Minor, August 1990
Suggested tune	FRANCONIA by Henry Havergal; or DONCASTER by Samuel Wesley

The short hymn has a valued place in congregational worship, as can be seen by the usefulness, for example, of Christopher Wordsworth's 'Lord, be thy Word my rule' or Joseph Hart's ' How good is the God we adore'. I did not begin this text with a marriage hymn in mind; but the three triplets (way, truth, life; faith, hope, charity; love, joy, peace) together with the trinitarian reference, seem to make it suitable as a hymn to ask God's blessing on a marriage.

LORD OF OUR LIVES, OUR BIRTH AND BREATH 86 86 (CM)

Theme	The Christian hope; death; a funeral
Written	at Ruan Minor, August 1990
Suggested tune	CONTEMPLATION by Frederick Arthur Gore Ouseley; or

CAITHNESS from the *Scottish Psalter*, Edinburgh 1635; *or* THEOC by Gordon Lawson

Published in   *New Songs of Praise 6*, 1991 to THEOC

A previous text was designated as 'suitable for a marriage' (see p.25) and with that in mind I sought soon afterwards to write a companion-piece, 'suitable for a funeral'. I would be glad to think it might be sung at mine.

The thought moves from an acknowledgment of God as our Creator and Sustainer in whose hands we rest, and to whom we bring our prayers and praises, through a thankful recollection of life past and an affirmation of Christian assurance. It concludes with a prayer for ourselves, the worshippers, in the days that are left to us. The hymn was first sung in the BBC TV programme 'Songs of Praise' in January 1991 from Cheadle, Cheshire.

MY DAYS OF WAITING ENDED   76 76 D

Based on	Psalm 40. 1-3
Theme	Deliverance; testimony; praise & worship
Written	at Ruan Minor and Poldhu Cove, August 1989
Suggested tune	PENLAN by David Jenkins

Psalm 40, verse 3 was among three passages of Scripture that met the eye of Charles Wesley at the time of his conversion to Christ on May 21st, 1738. 'I rose and looked into the Scripture' he wrote in his journal, followed by 'I now found myself at peace with God, and rejoiced in the hope of loving Christ.'

The verses link together the thoughts of deliverance and rejoicing which are so strongly marked in the life and work of Charles Wesley. His 'new triumphant songs' are songs of deliverance from 'the mire and shifting sand', reminiscent of Jeremiah's experience (Jeremiah 38.6f).

NOW IS CHRIST RISEN FROM THE DEAD   88 44 88
                                                    and Alleluias

Theme	Easter
Written	at Ford, April 1992
Suggested tune	EASTER SONG (German traditional)

'Alleluia', translated as 'Praise the Lord', comes in a number of the

Psalms, and four times in Revelation 19 as part of the heavenly song. Because it expresses joy, the Christian church has long linked its use in liturgy with Eastertide. EASTER SONG (also known as LASST UNS ERFREUEN and as ST FRANCIS) with its repeated Alleluias was originally associated with an Easter text; and more recently has been set to others on the same theme, for example to 'I know that my Redeemer lives' by Samuel Medley, or to 'Light's glittering morn bedecks the sky', a translation from the Latin by J. M. Neale. These texts come to us from the 18th and 19th centuries respectively, whereas the tune itself is 17th century.

The opening line of each stanza will have a familiar ring to those who recognize it as a direct quote from the AV version of 1 Corinthians 15.20, the opening of the set lesson at the Order for the Burial of the Dead in the *Book of Common Prayer*.

I have marked the text as 88 44 88, to fit EASTER SONG. But the Alleluias are not an integral part of the sense and meaning (as they are, for example, in 'Hear how the bells of Christmas play', *Songs of Deliverance* p.23), and the text can therefore be sung, without the Alleluias, to tunes in Long Metre.

O GOD OF EVERLASTING LIGHT   86 86 D (DCM)

Based on   John 3.3-16

Theme   The new birth

Written   at Ruan Minor, August 1990; and at Bramerton,
                     February 1990 and August 1991

Suggested tune   KINGSFOLD (traditional); *or*
                     FOREST GREEN (traditional); *or*
                     CLONMELL (Irish traditional)

In January 1990 I was asked by the hymnal committee of the First Christian Church, Columbus, Indiana for 'a versification of the first part of chapter 3 in the Gospel of John'. As can be seen from the dates above, the text took time to write; and in its final form does not wholly meet that description. It is due to appear in the hymnal which commissioned it during 1993.

O GOD WHO BROUGHT THE LIGHT TO BIRTH   88 88 88

Based on   Genesis 1-3

Theme   Creation; the fall

Written   at Ruan Minor, August 1990

Suggested tune	ABINGDON by Erik Routley; or
	MALLORY by William Jensen Reynolds; or
	PATER OMNIUM by Henry James Ernest Holmes
Published in	*100 Hymns of Hope*, 1992 to MALLORY

This text, like the last, was commissioned by Dan McKinley, organist and choirmaster of the First Christian Church, Columbus, Indiana. His letter to me of January 1990 said 'We have not found an appropriate hymn dealing with the first chapter, or the first three chapters, of Genesis. Thus our Hymn Number One - as the hymnal now stands - will be from Exodus 15, not Genesis. Somehow this seems incomplete...!'

The first three chapters of the Bible are of course particularly rich in setting out origins which go far beyond the bare facts of God's creation of our world. These verses contain references (echoed in this text) to the creation of light, space, galaxies, the solar system, vegetable, animal and then human life. 'Humankind' is shown as having dominion and sharing God's delight in creative powers. The institution of marriage, and of the principle of a cycle of work and rest, are alluded to in verse 3; while verse 4 goes beyond the first hint of the corruption of nature and the loss of innocence (verse 3, line 4) to sin's enslavement and the entail of shame and bondage.

The final verse extrapolates from the Genesis 3.15 reference (line 1) to the realization in Christ of this promise of redemption; and in the final line to its realization in Christian experience.

Christians have been accused of making the reference to 'dominion' in Genesis 1.26 a theological basis for the ruthless exploitation of the earth's natural resources. The text is careful in v.2 to link the 'dominion' given to humanity with a responsible stewardship over all the creation, of which we ourselves are part.

The closing couplet in each verse is intended to relate the objective facts of revelation to the subjective needs and experience of the worshipper - hence the sub-title, 'a meditation'.

O GOD WHOSE THOUGHTS ARE NOT AS OURS   86 86 D (DCM)

Theme	God the Father, the living God
Written	at Ruan Minor, August 1988
Suggested tune	ST MATTHEW by William Croft

The opening line is an echo of Isaiah 55. 8,9; and the hymn goes on to speak of God known in his works (earth, nature, the universe and an eternal world beyond); in his messengers (Sinai, the prophets, God's revealed nature); and, beyond all works and words, in his Son. He is a God of power, of righteousness, and of love.

The final phrase of verse 1, 'the edges of his ways' is borrowed from the title of a book by Amy Carmichael of Dohnavur, echoing Job 26.14, '... the outskirts of his ways'. 'The sum of things', is borrowed from A. E. Housman (in 'Epitaph on an army of mercenaries') who borrowed it from Milton.

PEACE BE YOURS AND DREAMLESS SLUMBER   8 33 6

Theme	Christmas
Written	at Ruan Minor, August 1989
Suggested tune	THANET by Joseph Jowett
Published in	*News of Hymnody*, October 1989 (words only)

'Blessings without number' is a phrase used by Isaac Watts in his 'Cradle Hymn', which first appeared in the eighth edition (1727) of *Divine Songs*, his celebrated collection for children first published in 1715. Here too the rhyme is with 'slumber'. I mention this because it is, I think, all that remains of a text which, in its first draft, read like a direct plagiarism of Watts - though quite unconsciously. I had wanted to write to the tune THANET (commended by Erik Routley[1]) and felt the particular metre and style of the tune very suitable for a Christmas lullaby. My opening line was therefore 'Hush you, Child, lie still and slumber'. I finished the text and put it away.

Ten days later, sitting on the beach on holiday and dipping into my battered copy of the *Oxford Book of English Verse*, I turned to the index to see what, if anything, Quiller-Couch had included of Watts and Wesley. There is in fact in the 1918 edition no Wesley and only two Watts. One of these is the 'Cradle Hymn' which begins 'Hush! my dear, lie still and slumber...' and continues 'Heavenly blessings without number...' No doubt I had read it before; but I had no inkling that what I had written was anything but original.

As can be seen, both the metre and the theme of this text differ from 'A Cradle Hymn' (which is a nursery song of some fourteen verses, addressed to any child at bedtime). But the episode remains in my mind as an illustration of how a line that 'sounds right' may in fact do so because it is already in use elsewhere. 'Emptied' in verse 2 is an allusion to Philippians 2.7.

1. Erik Routley, *I'll praise my Maker*, London 1951, p. 250

SO THE DAY DAWN FOR ME   64 64

Theme	Morning; trust in God
Written	at Ruan Minor and at Poldhu Cove, August 1988
Suggested tune	RAPHAEL by Kenneth Donald Smith; *or* STANGMORE by Donald Davison; *or* DONEYDADE by Donald Davison
Published in	*New Songs of Praise 6*, 1991 to (l.) STANGMORE; (2.) DONEYDADE

As sometime happens, this is a text that came without my seeking it, when in the middle of writing to a quite different metre and on a different theme. I noted in my MS book: 'I imagine a lilting Irish tune'; and was pleased to discover that there is a choice of tunes to this metre - in fact some five or six, not counting those which are really 10 10.

Because I felt there was something of a celtic 'feel' to the text, I sent it to Bishop Edward Darling, General Editor of *Irish Church Praise*; and he in turn passed it to W. Donald Davison, one of the music editors, who wrote for it the two new tunes to which it appears in *New Songs of Praise 6*.

THE BEST OF GIFTS IS OURS   66 86 (SM)

Based on	Philippians 4. 4-9
Theme	The Christian mind; peace & blessing
Written	at Ruan Minor and Gwithian beach, August 1990
Suggested tune	VENICE by William Amps; *or* NARENZA adapted by William Henry Havergal; *or* DAY OF PRAISE by Charles Steggall

The text seeks to include the well-known elements of Philippians 4.8 ('Whatsoever things are true...honest...just...') from a number of translations of the passage. The first two stanzas of the text refer to earlier verses of Paul's exhortation, starting at 'Rejoice in the Lord always...' and continuing with his v.7, often used as a liturgical blessing in the form 'The peace of God, which passes all understanding, keep your hearts and minds...' as in the *Book of Common Prayer*.

'The mind of Christ' in the final stanza is a Pauline expression (1 Corinthians 2.16) though not found in so many words in this passage. The metaphor of 'God's garden' is borrowed from the idea of the Spirit's fruit in Galatians 5.22.

THE CHURCH OF GOD ON EARTH, WE COME   87 87 887

Theme	The church; new life in Christ; the call of God
Written	at Ruan Minor, and Poldhu and Gwithian beaches, August 1990
Suggested tune	LUTHER (German traditional); *or* JENSEN by Willian Jensen Reynolds
Published in	*100 Hymns of Hope*, 1992 to JENSEN

The metre is not as unusual as it might appear at first sight. *Hymns and Tunes Indexed* by David Perry (Croydon, 1980) - that invaluable work of reference - gives 34 tunes. The hymn develops the thought of the church as God's new community, a community of love because it is the community of Jesus Christ.

THE LOVE OF CHRIST, WHO DIED FOR ME   86 86 (CM)

Theme	Passiontide; dedication & renewal; response to the gospel
Written	at Ruan Minor and Kennack sands, August 1989
Suggested tune	STRACATHRO by Charles Hutcheson; *or* AZMON by Carl Gotthelf Gläser
Published in	*Mission Praise* (combined edition), 1990 to a tune by Phil Burt *The Baptist Hymnal* (USA), 1991 to AZMON

In seeking to write a hymn of response to the gospel a few years ago (in 1987, at the suggestion of Canon Mark Ruston: see 'Above the voices of the world around me', *Songs of Deliverance* p. 5) I made the mistake of using a metre which severely limited any choice of well-known tune. So for this text I planned to write in CM - though these stanzas could be sung as well (or better) in DCM, were a really suitable tune to suggest itself for a particular congregation.

Although I have not indicated that the text is 'based on' any identifiable passage of Scripture, Galatians 2.20 with its reference to 'the Son of God, who loved me and gave himself up for me' is never far away.

THE PILGRIM CHURCH OF GOD   66 84 D

Based on	Ephesians 4.13

Theme	Pilgrimage
Suggested tune	LEONI (Hebrew melody)

In December 1987 the Bible Institute of Singapore asked me to try my hand at writing for them a College Hymn. Their motto, from Ephesians 4.13, is 'Unity, Knowledge, Perfection'; and the long seventh line of each stanza refers to these in turn. They then come together in the final verse as 'love and truth and grace', since love leads to unity, truth to knowledge, and grace to perfection in the world to come.

TO GOD OUR GREAT SALVATION 76 76 D

Based on	Psalm 145
Theme	Praise & worship
Written	at Bramerton, May 1988
Suggested tune	CRÜGER by Johann Crüger
Published in	*Psalms for Today*, 1990 to CRÜGER

Derek Kidner in his commentary (*Psalms 73-150*, IVP 1975) calls this psalm 'a great outpouring of worship' and says of the last doxology (verse 21):

> 'So ends David's contribution to the Psalter, on a note of praise which is wholly his own (21a), yet as wide as mankind and as unfading as eternity.'

I have tried to echo this inspiring exposition in my last four lines, by including the personal ('our hearts...'), the worldwide ('his earth...'), and the eternal ('for evermore...'). The word 'again' - the final word of the last line but one - is both a useful and a difficult word to rhyme. Useful, because it can be paired (to my ear, at least) with two distinct rhymes: for example, with 'pane' and 'pen'. But where it forms the first of the rhyming pair, its pronunciation has to be controlled by a word which is still (in singing or reading) at least a full line ahead. In this instance, it seems to me important that 'again' be given the shorter form of the second syllable, to secure a satisfying final rhyme.

TO GOD WHO GAVE THE SCRIPTURES 76 76 D

Theme	The Bible
Written	at Ruan Minor, August 1990
Suggested tune	EWING by Alexander Ewing; *or*

ELLACOMBE (German traditional); *or*
CRÜGER by Johann Crüger

Published in   *Celebrate the Growing* (Australia), 1991 to CRÜGER
            Bible Society Hymns, 1991 (words only)

In March 1990 the publishing manager of Scripture Union Australia wrote
to ask if I would attempt a hymn to accompany the launch of a new initiative
in Bible-reading notes, planned for 1991. This text is the result.

It contains a variety of allusions to, or echoes of, the text of scripture. For
example 2 Timothy 3.16; Psalm 119.105; Ephesians 4.12; Matthew 4.4;
Luke 8.11; Psalm 119.18; 1 Peter 1.25; Romans 10.17; Jeremiah 23.29; Luke
24.32; Luke 4.22; 1 Corinthians 15.3,4; Psalm 19.10; Ezekiel 3.3; Psalm
119.162; John 5.39; Luke 24.27.

WE BELIEVE IN GOD THE FATHER   87 87 or 87 87 D

Based on   The Apostles' Creed

Theme   Creed; testimony; trust in God

Written   at Ruan Minor, August 1989

Suggested tune   LUX EOI by Arthur Seymour Sullivan; *or*
            ALLELUIA by Samuel Sebastian Wesley; *or*
            ABBOT'S LEIGH by Cyril Vincent Taylor

Published in   *Sing to the Lord,* 1993 to RIPLEY arranged
            by Lowell Mason

In October 1988 the Ven. B. T. Lloyd, Archdeacon of Barnstaple and
Chairman of the Urban Priority Area working group of the Church of
England Liturgical Commission, wrote to ask for a metrical version of the
creed which could be sung to a standard hymn tune. There are, of course,
a number of hymns affirming basic Christian doctrines (for example, John
Henry Newman's 'Firmly I believe and truly') but few are close enough to
a traditional and universal creed for particular liturgical use.

This attempt is based on the version of the Apostles' Creed used in the
Alternative Services Book, 1989 of the Church of England, following that of
the International Consultation on English Texts. Their proposals on
creeds and canticles 'ultimately secured general acceptance in English-
speaking churches.' (*A Companion to the Alternative Service Book,* London
1986). I have included the ICET text of the Apostles' Creed[1] on the same
page as my text, to help those considering such a metrical version to compare it with an authorized liturgical original.

1. © 1970, 71, 75, by ICET reproduced by permission of the Central Board of
Finance of the Church of England.

WE TURN IN FAITH TO CHRIST THE LAMB OF GOD
10 4 10 4 10 10

Theme	Passiontide; redemption; the Lord Jesus Christ; response to the gospel
Written	At Bramerton, August 1991
Suggested tune	SANDON by Charles Henry Purday; or ALBERTA by Willam Henry Harris

The text builds on the framework of the second of the versions of Agnus Dei in the Holy Communion Rite A of the *Alternative Service Book*, 1980. This is itself an ICET text (see note above), the work of the late Dr J. G. Cuming. The text was written at the request of Simon Reynolds, to carry his tune CAER MENAI, as yet unpublished.

WHAT COLOURS GOD HAS MADE
66 86 (SM)

Theme	for children; creation; the love of God
Written	at Bramerton, February 1990
Suggested tune	COLORBURST by William Jensen Reynolds; or SOUTHWELL from William Damon's *Psalmes*, 1599; or SANDYS from William Sandys' *Christmas Carols Ancient and Modern*, 1833
Published in	*100 Hymns of Hope*, 1992 to COLORBURST *Anthem* by Austin Lovelace, Selah Publishing Co., USA 1992

The text, for children, attempts to weave the theme of colour into that of the changing seasons. It was written for the Recorder Group of Thorpe Hamlet First School, Norwich, at the request of their teacher, and dedicated to her daughter Rachel Codling, a member of the group. They had been learning the tune SOUTHWELL, but finding the familiar words 'Lord Jesus, think on me, by many a care oppressed...' inappropriate for six-to-eight-year-olds in school. The Norfolk Agreed Syllabus of Religious Education includes for this age-range ideas of exploring experience through the natural world and through the Bible; and this text is an attempt to link the two, together with 'the Christian belief that everyone is special to God.'

WHEN THE WAY IS HARD TO FIND
77 77 77

Theme	Guidance; pilgrimage; the Bible; trust in God
Written	at Ruan Minor, August 1988
Suggested tune	WELLSPRING by D. S. Bortnianski,

The text seeks to affirm the reality of God's guidance, in accordance with his many promises, to those who are willing to obey the light given. Verse 2 speaks of the 'human predicament', in the image of the trackless ocean (to the ancient Jews, a particularly hostile environment), calling forth the prayer of faith. Verse 3 suggests God's guidance through scripture and the inner witness of the Spirits's voice; while in the final verse 'the light of Christ' is accompanied by faith, confidence, peace and progress.

INDEXES

- HYMNALS
- BIBLICAL REFERENCES
- METRE
- SUGGESTED TUNES
- SUBJECTS, CUMULATIVE
- FIRST LINES, CUMULATIVE
- SUBJECTS
- FIRST LINES

The two indexes marked 'cumulative' above refer not only to this book, but also to texts found in *Lift Every Heart* and in *Songs of Deliverance*. They thus form a complete subject index, and a complete index of first lines, to all my hymn texts up to August 1992.

TDS

Index of hymnals

published or in preparation, containing hymns in this collection.

Two new hymns in celebration of Christingle, Children's Society, London 1989
God whose love is everywhere

Mission Praise (combined edition), Marshall Pickering, London 1990
Christ the Way of life possess me
Come, watch with us this Christmas night
Freely, for the love he bears us
The love of Christ, who died for me

New Songs of Praise 5, Oxford University Press/BBC, Oxford 1990
God whose love is everywhere

Psalms for Today, Hodder & Stoughton, London 1990
To God our great salvation

The Baptist Hymnal, Convention Press, Nashville, USA 1991
How great our God's majestic Name!
The love of Christ, who died for me

Bible Sunday Hymns, Bible Society, Swindon 1991
To God who gave the scriptures

Celebrate the Growing, Scripture Union Australia, Melbourne 1991
To God who gave the scriptures

The Popular Carol Book, Mowbray, London 1991
Child of Mary, newly born

The Promise of His Glory, Mowbray/Church House Publishing, London 1991
God whose love is everywhere

New Songs of Praise 6, Oxford University Press/BBC, Oxford 1991
Child of Mary, newly born
Lord of our lives, our birth and breath
So the day dawn for me

100 Hymns of Hope, Hope Publishing Co., Carol Stream, USA 1992
O God who brought the light to birth
The church of God on earth, we come
What colours God has made

Sing to the Lord, Lillenas Publishing Company, Kansas City, USA 1993
We believe in God the Father

Periodicals

Christian Music,	Autumn 1989 (Herald House Ltd. & Music in Worship Trust)
	Come, watch with us this Christmas night
News of Hymnody,	August 1989 (Grove Books Ltd.)
	Peace be yours and dreamless slumber
New Song,	September 1992 (Hope Publishing Co., USA)
	Here is the centre: star on distant star

What colours God has made
to music by Austin Lovelace, Selah Publishing Co. USA 1992

Child of Mary, newly born
to music by Austin Lovelace, Kenwood Press Ltd., USA 1992

Index of Biblical References

Please see the Foreword for further details

Genesis	1-3	O God who brought the light to birth
1 Kings	8.22f	Draw near to God, whose steadfast love
Psalm	8	How great our God's majestic Name!
Psalm	34	All our days we will bless the Lord
Psalm	40.1-3	My days of waiting ended
Psalm	100	Let the earth acclaim him
Psalm	145	To God our great salvation
Proverbs		Christ the Way of life possess me
Isaiah	55.8,9	O God whose thoughts are not as ours
John		Christ is the Bread of life indeed
John	3.3-16	O God of everlasting light
1 Corinthians	15.20	Now is Christ risen from the dead
Galatians	2.20	The love of Christ, who died for me
Ephesians	4.13	The pilgrim church of God
Philippians	4.4-9	The best of gifts is ours

From the Alternative Service Book, 1980 of the Church of England:

| Apostles' Creed | We believe in God the Father |

From the Rite A Holy Communion Service:

| Acclamations | Freely, for the love he bears us |
| Agnus Dei | We turn in faith to Christ the Lamb of God |

Metrical Index

64 64
So the day dawn for me

6665 D
Let the earth acclaim him

6666 4444
Christ is the One who calls

66 84 D
The pilgrim church of God

66 86 (Short Metre: SM)
Lord, hear us as we pray
The best of gifts is ours
What colours God has made

76 76 D
My days of waiting ended
To God our great salvation
To God who gave the scriptures

7775 775
God whose love is everywhere

77 77 77
When the way is hard to find

77 77 D
Child of Mary, newly born

8 33 6
Peace be yours and dreamless slumber

86 86 (Common Metre: CM)
Draw near to God, whose steadfast love
Lord of our lives, our birth and breath
The love of Christ, who died for me

86 86 D (Double Common Metre: DCM)
Come, watch with us this Christmas
  night
O God of everlasting light
O God whose thoughts are not as ours

87 83
Christ the Way of life possess me

87 85
Freely, for the love he bears us

87 87
We believe in God the Father
  (or 87 87 D)

87 87 87
Christ who called disciples to him

87 87 D
Christ is come! Let earth adore him
We believe in God the Father (or 87 87)

87 87 887
The church of God on earth, we come

88 44 88 and Alleluias
Now is Christ risen from the dead

8884
Christ is the Bread of life indeed
Lord, for the gift of this new day

88 88 (Long Metre: LM)
How great our God's majestic Name!
(Now is Christ risen from the dead)

88 88 88
All our days we will bless the Lord
O God who brought the light to birth

10 4 10 4 10 10
We turn in faith to Christ the Lamb of
  God

10 10 10 10
As in that upper room you left your
  seat
God is not far, whose threefold mercies
  shine

10 10 10 10 10 10
Here is the centre: star on distant star

11 11 11 11
God lies beyond us, throned in light
  resplendent

Index of suggested tunes

Tunes to which texts have been set in the published hymnals
listed on page 68 are marked*

ABBOT'S LEIGH
Christ is come! Let earth adore him
We believe in God the Father

ABERYSTWYTH
Child of Mary, newly born

ABINGDON
O God who brought the light to birth

ALBERTA
We turn in faith to Christ the Lamb of
God

ALLELUIA
Christ is come! Let earth adore him
We believe in God the Father

*ASHLANDS
Here is the centre: star on distant star

*AZMON
The love of Christ, who died for me

CAITHNESS
Lord of our lives, our birth and breath

*CHRISTMAS NIGHT
Come, watch with us this Christmas
night

CLONMELL
O God of everlasting light

*COLORBURST
What colours God has made

CONTEMPLATION
Lord of our lives, our birth and breath

*CRÜGER
To God our great salvation
To God who gave the scriptures

DAY OF PRAISE
The best of gifts is ours

DONCASTER
Lord, hear us we pray

*DONEYDADE
So the day dawn for me

DOVERSDALE
How great our Gods's majestic Name!

*DUKE STREET
How great our God's majestic Name!

EASTER SONG
Now is Christ risen from the dead

EISENACH
How great our God's majestic Name!

ES IST KEIN TAG
Christ is the Bread of life indeed
Lord, for the gift of this new day

*FALLING FIFTHS
God whose love is everywhere

FOREST GREEN
O God of everlasting light

FRANCONIA
Lord, hear us as we pray

GRIFFIN'S BROOK
Freely for the love he bears us

HERE AND NOW
Here is the centre; star on distant star

HOBART HIGH
God is not far, whose threefold mercies
shine

HORNSEY
Christ the Way of life possess me

*JENSEN
The church of God on earth, we come

JULIUS
God is not far, whose threefold mercies
shine

KINGSFOLD
O God of everlasting light
Come, watch with us this Christmas
night

LEONI
The pilgrim church of God

LINGWOOD
Christ who called disciples to him

LODDON
God lies beyond us, throned in light
resplendent

LOVE UNKNOWN
Christ is the One who calls

LUTHER
The church of God on earth, we come

LUX EOI
We believe in God the Father

*LYNCH'S LULLABY
Child of Mary, newly born

MAIDSTONE
Child of Mary, newly born

*MALLORY
O God who brought the light to birth

NARENZA
The best of gifts is ours

NOEL
Come, watch with us this Christmas
night

NONINGTON
Christ the Way of life possess me

PATER OMNIUM
O God who brought the light to birth

PENLAN
My days of waiting ended

PORTLAND
Christ is the Bread of life indeed

RAPHAEL
So the day dawn for me

REGENT SQUARE
Christ who called disciples to him

RHUDDLAN
Christ who called disciples to him

RICHMOND
Draw near to God, whose steadfast love

*RIPLEY
We believe in God the Father

RIPPONDEN
Christ is the Bread of life indeed

ST MATTHEW
O God whose thoughts are not as ours

SANDON
We turn in faith to Christ the Lamb of
God

SANDYS
What colours God has made

SONG 1
Here is the centre: star on distant star

SONG 22
As in that upper room you left your
seat

SOUTHWELL
What colours God has made

*STANGMORE
So the day dawn for me

STRACATHRO
The love of Christ, who died for me

THANET
Peace be yours and dreamless slumber

*THEOC
Lord of our lives, our birth and breath

VENICE
The best of gifts is ours

VIGIL
Christ the Way of life possess me

WELLSPRING
When the way is hard to find

I maintain a file of MS music sent to me by composers who have written tunes to my
texts, and will gladly send details to editors or others who may wish to consult it.

TDS

Cumulative index of subjects

of the texts in all three collections, *Lift Every Heart* (L), *Songs of Deliverance* (S) and *A Voice of Singing* (A). The letter in brackets after each text below denotes the book which includes the text.

Advent
(See also: Christmas & Epiphany)
Freely, for the love he bears us (A)
From the Father's throne on high (S)
When he comes (L)
When the Lord in glory comes (L)

Anniversary
(See also: Thanksgiving)
Give thanks to God on high (S)
Here within this house of prayer (L)
Lord, for the years your love has kept and guided (L)
O Christ the same, through all our story's pages (L)

Armour of God
Be strong in the Lord (L)

Ascension
Christ high-ascended, now in glory seated (L)
He walks among the golden lamps (L)
Name of all majesty (L)
Saviour Christ (L)
Thankful of heart for days gone by (L)

Baptism
(See also: Call of God; Church membership & confirmation; Dedication of a child)
Father, now behold us (L)
Now to the Lord we bring the child he gave us (L)
This child from God above (L)
We turn to Christ anew (L)
When John baptised by Jordan's river (L)

Bible
God of old, whom saints and sages (L)
O Christ, who taught on earth of old (L)
The pilgrim church of God (A)
The will of God to mark my way (L)
To God who gave the scriptures (A)
When the way is hard to find (A)

Blessing
See: Peace & blessing

Call of God
(See also: Response to the gospel)
Christ is the One who calls (A)
Christ who called disciples to him (A)
O changeless Christ, for ever new (L)
The church of God on earth, we come (A)
We come as guests invited (L)
We turn to Christ anew (L)

Children, suitable for
Bless the Lord, creation sings (S)
Christ be my leader by night as by day (L)
Donkey plod and Mary ride (L)
God whose love is everywhere (A)
Hush you, my baby (L)
Jesus is the Lord of living (L)
So the day dawn for me (A)
Soft the evening shadows fall (S)
What colours God has made (A)

Christ our Light
Christ be the Lord of all our days (L)
Christ is the Bread of life indeed (A)
From the night of ages waking (S)
Light of the minds that know him (L)
To Christ our King in songs of praise (L)
We sing the Lord our light (L)

Christian experience & discipleship
(See also: Lord Jesus Christ; New life in Christ; Pilgrimage)
Christ be my leader by night as by day (L)
Christ be the Lord of all our days (L)
Christ the Way of life possess me (A)
Christ who called disciples to him (A)
Father of lights, who brought to birth (L)
Father who formed the family of man (L)
Jesus my breath, my life, my Lord (L)
Light of the minds that know him (L)
Lord of our lives, our birth and breath (A)
No temple now, no gift of price (L)
O changeless Christ, for ever new (L)
O Christ the same, through all our story's pages (L)
O come to me, the Master said (S)
To Christ our King in songs of praise (L)
We turn to Christ anew (L)

Christian hope
(See also: Advent; Death; Easter)
Beloved in Christ before our life began (S)
Lord of our lives, our birth and breath (A)
Within the love of God I hide (S)

Christian mind
The best of gifts is ours (A)

Christian year
(See: Advent; Christmas & Epiphany;
    Palm Sunday; Passiontide; Eastertide;
    Ascension; Pentecost; Trinity;
    Transfiguration; Embertide; Harvest.)

Christingle
God whose love is everywhere (A)

Christmas & Epiphany
—A song was heard at Christmas (L)
Child of Mary, newly born (A)
—Child of the stable's secret birth (L)
— Chill of the nightfall (L)
Christ from heaven's glory come (L)
Christ is come! Let earth adore him (A)
—Come now with awe, earth's ancient
    vigil keeping (L)
— Come, watch with us this Christmas
    night (A)
Donkey plod and Mary ride (L)
Had he not loved us (L)
Hear how the bells of Christmas play! (S)
Here is the centre: star on distant star (A)
High peaks and sunlit prairies (L)
—Holy child, how still you lie (L)
— How faint the stable-lantern's light (L)
—Hush you, my baby (L)
—Not in lordly state and splendour (L)
O child of Mary, hark to her (L)
— O Prince of peace whose promised
    birth (L)
Peace be yours and dreamless
    slumber (A)
— See, to us a child is born (L)
—Soft the evening shadows fall (S)
Stars of heaven, clear and bright (L)
—The darkness turns to dawn (L)
The King of glory comes to earth (S)
—The shining stars unnumbered (L)
Where do Christmas songs begin? (S)
Within a crib my Saviour lay (L)

Church
(See also: Holy Communion)
Born by the Holy Spirit's breath (L)

Here within this house of prayer (L)
Look, Lord, in mercy as we pray (L)
Lord of the church, we pray for our
    renewing (L)
Servants of the living Lord (L)
The church of God on earth, we come (A)
The faithful are kept as the mountains (S)
The pilgrim church of God (A)
When God the Spirit came (L)

Church membership & confirmation
(See also: Baptism; Christian experience
    & discipleship; Dedication & renewal)
Christ the Way of life possess me (A)
Christ who called disciples to him (A)
We turn in faith to Christ the Lamb of
    God (A)
We turn to Christ anew (L)
When John baptised by Jordan's river (L)

Church's year
See: Christian year

Citizens of heaven
See: Heaven

Confidence & peace
(See also: Faith; God our strength;
    Peace & blessing; Peace of the world;
    Trust in God)
All our days we will bless the Lord (A)
All shall be well (L)
God is my great desire (L)
I lift my eyes to the quiet hills (L)
'Set your troubled hearts at rest' (L)
The will of God to mark my way (L)
Within the love of God I hide (S)

Confirmation
See: Church membership &
    confirmation

Creation
(See also: Harvest)
All flowers of garden, field and hill (L)
Bless the Lord, creation sings (S)
How great our God's majestic Name! (A)
In endless exultation (L)
O God who brought the light to birth (A)
The heavens are singing, are singing
    and praising (L)
The Lord in wisdom made the earth (L)
The stars declare his glory (L)
What colours God has made (A)

Creed
We believe in God the Father

Cross of Christ
See: Passiontide

Death
(See also: Eastertide)
Christ be the Lord of all our days (L)
Christ is the Bread of life indeed (A)
Faithful vigil ended (L)
Jesus my breath, my life, my Lord (L)
Lighten our darkness now the day is
  ended (L)
Lord of our lives, our birth and breath (A)
O Christ the same, through all our
  story's pages (L)
'Set your troubled hearts at rest' (L)

Dedication & renewal
(See also: Response to the gospel)
Give thanks to God on high (L)
Look, Lord, in mercy as we pray (L)
Lord, for the years your love has kept
  and guided (L)
Lord of the church, we pray for our
  renewing (L)
O Saviour Christ, beyond all price (L)
The love of Christ who died for me (A)
We turn in faith to Christ the Lamb of
  God (A)
We turn to Christ anew (L)

Dedication of a child
(see also: Baptism)
This cherished child of God's creation (S)

Deliverance
(See also: Redemption)
Faithful vigil ended (L)
From all the wind's wide quarters (S)
In my hour of grief or need (L)
Living Lord, our praise we render (L)
Lighten our darkness now the day is
  ended (L)
My days of waiting ended (A)
Safe in the shadow of the Lord (L)
Tell his praise in song and story (L)
The love of Christ, who died for me (A)

Discipleship
See: Christian experience & discipleship

Eastertide
All shall be well (L)
And sleeps my Lord in silence yet (L)
By loving hands the Lord is laid (L)

Christ is risen as he said (S)
Come and see where Jesus lay (S)
Freely, for the love he bears us (A)
From afar a cock is crowing (L)
Jesus, Prince and Saviour (L)
Living Lord, our praise we render (L)
Long before the world is waking (L)
Now is Christ risen from the dead (A)
This day above all days (L)
Who is there on this Easter morning (L)

Embertide
(See also: Ministry)
Lord, give us eyes to see (L)

Epiphany
See: Christmas & Epiphany

Evangelism
See: Mission & evangelism

Evening
Bless the Lord as day departs (L)
Faithful vigil ended (L)
Lighten our darkness now the day is
  ended (L)
So the day dawn for me (A)

Faith
(See also: Call of God; Confidence &
  peace; Creed; Trust in God)
Dear Lord, who bore our weight
  of woe (L)
Faithful vigil ended (L)
Freely, for the love he bears us (A)
God is my great desire (L)
God of eternal grace (L)
He comes to us as one unknown (L)
Here within this house of prayer (L)
Jesus, my breath, my life, my Lord (L)
No temple now, no gift of price (L)
O Saviour Christ, beyond all price (L)
Safe in the shadow of the Lord (L)
Spirit of faith, by faith be mine (S)
Tell his praise in song and story (L)
The faithful are kept as the mountains (S)
We turn in faith to Christ the Lamb
  of God (A)

Fall
O God who brought the light to birth (A)
The Lord made man, the scriptures
  tell (L)

Family
See: Home & family

Feast of life
From all the wind's wide quarters (S)

Flower festival
(See also: Creation; Harvest)
All flowers of garden, field and hill (L)

Fruit of the Spirit
(See also: Pentecost)
Fruitful trees, the Spirit's sowing (L)

Funeral
(See also: Death; Eastertide)
Lord of our lives, our birth and breath (A)

God our strength
(See also: Confidence & peace)
Be strong in the Lord (L)
God is my great desire (L)
God is not far, whose threefold mercies
    shine (A)
God lies beyond us, throned in light
    transcendent (A)
The faithful are kept as the mountains (S)
We sing the Lord our light (L)

God the Father, the living God
(See also: Lord Jesus Christ; Pentecost;
    Praise & worship; Trinity)
Draw near to God, whose steadfast
    love (A)
Father of lights, who brought to birth (L)
Father who formed the family of man (L)
God and Father, ever giving (S)
God is King! The Lord is reigning (L)
God of eternal grace (L)
God of gods, we sound his praises (L)
How great our God's majestic Name! (A)
Not to us be glory given (L)
O God whose thoughts are not as ours (A)
Our God eternal, reigning (S)
Servants of the living Lord (L)
Tell out, my soul, the greatness of the
    Lord (L)
The everlasting Lord is King (S)
The heavens are singing, are singing
    and praising (L)
Timeless love! We sing the story (L)
To God our great salvation (A)
To heathen dreams of human pride (L)

Gospel
(See also: Mission & evangelism; New
    life in Christ; Response to the gospel)
From all the wind's wide quarters (S)
From the night of ages waking (S)

Good news of God above (S)
Living Lord, our praise we render (L)
No weight of gold or silver (L)
O God of everlasting light (A)
Out of darkness let light shine (L)
The Lord made man, the scriptures
    tell (L)

Grace
(See also; Love of God; Redemption)
Almighty Lord Most High draw near (S)
Behold, as love made manifest (L)
God of eternal grace (L)
No temple now, no gift of price (L)
Servants of the living Lord (L)
The God of grace is ours (S)
To God our great salvation (A)

Guidance
The pilgrim church of God (A)
The will of God to mark my way (L)
When the way is hard to find (A)

Harvest
(See also: Creation; Thanksgiving)
All flowers of garden, field and hill (L)
Every heart its tribute pays (L)
Fill your hearts with joy and gladness (L)
Mercy, blessing, favour, grace (L)
O Christ, who taught on earth of old (L)

Healing
When to our world the Saviour came (L)

Heaven
(See also: Death; Eastertide)
A city radiant as a bride (S)
O changeless Christ, for ever new (L)
Lord of our lives, our birth and breath (A)

Holy Communion
(See also: Passiontide)
An upper room with evening lamps
    ashine (S)
As in that upper room you left your
    seat (A)
Christ is the Bread of life indeed (A)
O changeless Christ, for ever new (L)
O come to me, the Master said (S)
We come as guests invited (L)
When Jesus lived among us (L)

Holy Spirit
See: Pentecost

Holy Trinity
See: Trinity

Home & family
Father on high to whom we pray (L)
Lord, who left the highest heaven (L)

Hope
See: Christian hope

Incarnation
See: Christmas & Epiphany; Lord Jesus
    Christ

John the Baptist
When John baptised by Jordan's river (L)

Joy
See: Rejoicing

Judgment
Let every child of earth that sleeping
    lies (S)

Light
See: Christ our Light

Lord Jesus Christ
(See also: Christian year; Parables;
    Praise & worship; New life in Christ)
As water to the thirsty (L)
Christ be my leader by night as by day (L)
Christ is the Bread of life indeed (A)
Christ is the One who calls (A)
Freely, for the love he bears us (A)
He comes to us as one unknown (L)
He walks among the golden lamps (L)
Jesus is the Lord of living (L)
Jesus my breath, my life, my lord (L)
Let hearts and voices blend (L)
Light of the minds that know him (L)
Name of all majesty (L)
O changeless Christ, for ever new (L)
O Saviour Christ, beyond all price (L)
Our Saviour Christ once knelt in
    prayer (L)
Praise be to Christ in whom we see (L)
Saviour Christ (L)
The Lord is here! (S)
To Christ our King in songs of praise (L)
We turn in faith to Christ the Lamb of
    God (A)
When Jesus lived among us (L)
When John baptised by Jordan's river (L)
Who is Jesus? Friend of sinners (L)

Lord's Supper
See: Holy Communion

Love
Not for tongues of heaven's angels (S)

Love for God
For peace with God above (S)
God and Father, ever giving (S)
God is my great desire (L)
Jesus my breath, my life, my Lord (L)

Love of God
(See also: Christingle; Passiontide)
Beloved in Christ before our life began (S)
Born by the Holy Spirit's breath (L)
Eye has not seen, nor ear has heard (S)
Timeless love! We sing the story (L)
We sing the Lord our light (L)
What colours God has made (A)
Within the love of God I hide (S)

Marriage
At Cana's wedding, long ago (L)
Lord, hear us as we pray (A)

Ministry
'How shall they hear,' who have not
    heard (L)
Lord, give us eyes to see (L)
Servants of the living Lord (L)
When God the Spirit came (L)
When to our world the Saviour came (L)

Mission & evangelism
(See also: Response to the gospel;
    Social concern & the world's need)
Christ high-ascended, now in glory
    seated (L)
Christ is the One who calls (A)
Come and see where Jesus lay (S)
Good news of God above (S)
'How shall they hear,' who have not
    heard (L)
Look, Lord, in mercy as we pray (L)
Lord of the church, we pray for our
    renewing (L)
Tell out, my soul, the greatness of the
    Lord (L)
When God the Spirit came (L)
Who is Jesus? Friend of sinners (L)

Morning
Come, let us praise the Lord (L)
Lord, as the day begins (L)
Lord, for the gift of this new day (A)
So the day dawn for me (A)

National
(see also: Anniversary; Thanksgiving)
Lord, for the years your love has kept
and guided (L)

Nature
See: Creation

New birth
Born by the Holy Spirit's breath (L)
O God of everlasting light (A)

New life in Christ
(See also: Baptism; Dedication &
renewal; New birth)
Above the voices of the world around
me (S)
Christ the Way of life possess me (A)
Christ who called disciples to him (A)
Living Lord, our praise we render (L)
No weight of gold or silver (L)
Out of darkness let light shine (L)
The church of God on earth, we come (A)
The Lord made man, the scriptures tell (L)
We turn to Christ anew (L)
We turn in faith to Christ the Lamb of
God (A)

New Jerusalem
A city radiant as a bride (S)

Offertory
See: Dedication & renewal;
Stewardship; Thanksgiving

Ordination
See: Ministry

Palm Sunday
No tramp of soldiers' marching feet (L)

Parables
Christ is the Bread of life indeed (A)
O Christ, who taught on earth of old (L)

Passiontide
A purple robe, a crown of thorn (L)
Approach with awe this holiest place (S)
Behold, as love made manifest (L)
Dear Lord, who bore our weight of
woe (L)
No weight of gold or silver (L)
O Saviour Christ, beyond all price (L)
The love of Christ, who died for me (A)
We turn in faith to Christ the Lamb of
God (A)

Peace and blessing
(See also: Confidence & peace)
For peace with God above (S)
Lord, hear us as we pray (A)
O Prince of peace whose promised
birth (L)
'Set your troubled hearts at rest' (L)
Stars of heaven, clear and bright (L)
The best of gifts is ours (A)

Peace of the world
Behold a broken world, we pray (S)
O Prince of peace whose promised
birth (L)

Penitence
(See also: Response to the gospel)
Almighty Lord Most High draw near (S)
Dear Lord, who bore our weight of
woe (L)
The Lord made man, the scriptures
tell (L)

Pentecost
Be present, Spirit of the Lord (S)
Born by the Holy Spirit's breath (L)
Fruitful trees, the Spirit's sowing (L)
Spirit of faith, by faith be mine (S)
Spirit of God within me (L)
When God the Spirit came (L)

Pilgrimage
Christ be my leader by night as by day (L)
Christ the Way of life possess me (A)
Tell his praise in song and story (L)
The pilgrim church of God (A)
When the way is hard to find (A)

Praise & worship
All glory be to God on high (L)
All our days we will bless the Lord (A)
Beyond all mortal praise (L)
Bless the Lord, creation sings (S)
Come, let us praise the Lord (L)
Every heart its tribute pays (L)
Fill your hearts with joy and gladness (L)
Glory to God in the highest (L)
God and Father, ever giving (S)
God is King! The Lord is reigning (L)
God of eternal grace (L)
Heavenly hosts in ceaseless worship (L)
How great our God's majestic Name! (A)
In endless exultation (L)
Let the earth acclaim him (A)
Mercy, blessing, favour, grace (L)

My days of waiting ended (A)
Praise be to Christ in whom we see (L)
Praise the God of our salvation (L)
Praise the Lord and bless his name (S)
Praise the Lord of heaven (L)
Servants of the living Lord (L)
Sing a new song to the Lord (L)
Tell his praise in song and story (L)
Tell out, my soul, the greatness of the
   Lord (L)
The God of grace is ours (S)
The heavens are singing, are singing
   and praising (L)
The Lord is here! (S)
The stars declare his glory (L)
To God our great salvation (A)
Timeless love! We sing the story (L)

Prayer
(See also: Thanksgiving)
As for our world we lift our hearts in
   praise (L)
Father on high to whom we pray (L)
Father, who formed the family of man (L)
Here within this house of prayer (L)
Light of the minds that know him (L)
Look, Lord, in mercy as we pray (L)
Lord, hear us as we pray (A)
Lord of the church, we pray for our
   renewing (L)
O Lord, yourself declare (L)

Redemption
(See also: Christmas & Epiphany;
   Deliverance; Lord Jesus Christ;
   Passiontide)
All glory be to God on high (L)
Approach with awe this holiest place (S)
Dear Lord, who bore our weight of
   woe (L)
From all the wind's wide quarters (S)
Glory to God in the highest (L)
God of gods, we sound his praises (L)
Let hearts and voices blend (L)
Living Lord, our praise we render (L)
My days of waiting ended (A)
No temple now, no gift of price (L)
O God who brought the light to birth (A)
Our God and Father bless (S)
Praise the God of our salvation (L)
The heavens are singing, are singing
   and praising (L)
The love of Christ who died for me (A)
To God our great salvation (A)

We turn in faith to Christ the Lamb of
   God (A)

Rejoicing
(See also: Thanksgiving)
Bless the Lord, creation sings (S)
Come, let us praise the Lord (L)
Fill your hearts with joy and gladness (L)
Freely, for the love he bears us (A)
Good news of God above (S)
In endless exultation (L)
Let the earth acclaim him (A)
Sing a new song to the Lord (L)
So the day dawn for me (A)
The heavens are singing, are singing
   and praising (L)
The best of gifts is ours (A)

Renewal
See: Dedication & renewal

Response to the gospel
Above the voices of the world around
   me (S)
Christ who called disciples to him (A)
The love of Christ, who died for me (A)
We turn in faith to Christ the Lamb of
   God (A)

Resurrection
See: Eastertide; New life in Christ

Return of Christ in glory
See: Advent

Saints
Give thanks to God on high (S)

Scripture
See: Bible

Social concern & the world's need
As for our world we lift our hearts in
   praise (L)
Behold a broken world, we pray (S)
Christ from heaven's glory come (L)
Lord, who left the highest heaven (L)
Remember, Lord, the world you made (L)
When to our world the Saviour came (L)

Stewardship
(See also: Thanksgiving)
The God of grace is ours (S)

Sunday
This day above all days (L)

Testimony
Christ high-ascended, now in glory
  seated (L)
Come, let us praise the Lord (L)
My days of waiting ended (A)
Tell his praise in song and story (L)
We believe in God the Father (A)
Within the love of God I hide (S)

Thanksgiving
All glory be to God on high (L)
Fill your hearts with joy and gladness (L)
Give thanks to God on high (S)
God whose love is everywhere (A)
Here within this house of prayer (L)
Let the earth acclaim him (A)
Lord, for the years your love has kept
  and guided (L)
O Christ the same, through all our
  story's pages (L)
The God of grace is ours (S)
Praise the God of our salvation (L)
Thankful of heart for days gone by(L)

Transfiguration
Our Saviour Christ once knelt in
  prayer (L)

Trinity
All glory be to God on high (L)
Father on high to whom we pray (L)
Glory to God in the highest (L)
God and Father, ever giving (S)
God is not far, whose threefold mercies
  shine (A)
God lies beyond us, throned in light
  resplendent (A)
God of gods, we sound his praises (L)
Here within this house of prayer (L)

Trust in God
(See also: Confidence & peace)
All my soul to God I raise (L)
All our days we will bless the Lord (A)
Draw near to God, whose steadfast
  love (A)
Praise the Lord and bless his Name (S)
Safe in the shadow of the Lord (L)
So the day dawn for me (A)
We believe in God the Father (A)

Unity
Father on high to whom we pray (L)
Look, Lord, in mercy as we pray (L)
Lord of the church, we pray for our
  renewing (L)

Wedding
See: Marriage

Whitsun
See: Pentecost

Wisdom of God
Eye has not seen, nor ear has heard (S)
Father of lights, who brought to birth (L)
Praise be to Christ in whom we see (L)
The Lord in wisdom made the earth (L)

World
See: Mission & evangelism; Social
  concern & the world's need

Worship
See: Praise & worship

Youth
(See also: Church membership &
  confirmation)
Christ be my leader by night as by day (L)
Christ who called disciples to him (A)
Give thanks to God on high (S)
Jesus is the Lord of living (L)
Name of all majesty (L)
When he comes (L)
When the Lord in glory comes (L)

Cumulative index of first lines

The texts below, listed alphabetically by first line, combine all the hymn texts from the three collections shown, including this one. The first column shows the book, and the second and third the page number of Text and Note respectively.

Index of subjects

of the texts printed in this book.
New categories, not in *Lift Every Heart* or *Songs of Deliverance*, are marked *.
For cumulative index of subjects, see page 74.

Bible
The pilgrim church of God
To God who gave the scriptures
When the way is hard to find

*Call of God
Christ is the One who calls
Christ who called disciples to him
The church of God on earth, we come

*Children, suitable for
God whose love is everywhere
So the day dawn for me
What colours God has made

Christ our Light
Christ is the Bread of life indeed

Christian experience & discipleship
Christ the Way of life possess me
Christ who called disciples to him
Lord of our lives, our birth and breath

Christian hope
Lord of our lives, our birth and breath

*Christian mind
The best of gifts is ours

*Christian year
See: Christmas & Epiphany;
Passiontide; Eastertide; Holy Trinity

*Christingle
God whose love is everywhere

Christmas & Epiphany
Child of Mary, newly born
Christ is come! Let earth adore him
Come, watch with us this Christmas
  night
Here is the centre: star on distant star
Peace be yours and dreamless slumber

*Church
(See also: Holy Communion)
The church of God on earth, we come
The pilgrim church of God

*Church membership & confirmation
Christ who called disciples to him
We turn in faith to Christ the Lamb of
  God

Church's year
See: Christmas & Epiphany;
  Passiontide; Eastertide; Holy Trinity

Confidence & peace
(See also: Peace & blessing; Trust in
  God)
All our days we will bless the Lord
Within the love of God I hide

Creation
How great our God's majestic Name!
O God who brought the light to birth
What colours God has made

*Creed
We believe in God the Father

Cross
See: Passiontide

Death
(See also: Eastertide)
Christ is the Bread of life indeed
Lord, of our lives, our birth and breath

Dedication and renewal
(See also: Response to the gospel)
The love of Christ, who died for me
We turn in faith to Christ the Lamb of
  God

Deliverance
My days of waiting ended
The love of Christ, who died for me
To God our great salvation

Discipleship
See: Christian experience & discipleship

Eastertide
Freely, for the love he bears us
Now is Christ risen from the dead

Epiphany
See: Christmas & Epiphany

Evangelism
See: Mission & evangelism

Renewal
See: Dedication & renewal

Response to the gospel
Christ who called disciples to him
The love of Christ, who died for me
We turn in faith to Christ the Lamb of God

Resurrection
See: Eastertide

Scripture
See: Bible

Testimony
My days of waiting ended
We believe in God the Father

Thanksgiving
God whose love is everywhere
Let the earth acclaim him

Trinity
God is not far, whose threefold mercies
  shine
God lies beyond us, throned in light
  transcendent

Trust in God
(See also: Faith)
All our days we will bless the Lord
Draw near to God, whose steadfast love
So the day dawn for me
We believe in God the Father

Wedding
See: Marriage

Worship
See: Praise & worship

Youth
Christ who called disciples to him

Index of First Lines

of the texts printed in this book